TEN
VERSIONS
OF
AMERICA

1972

ALFRED A. KNOPF: New York

TEN
VERSIONS
OF
AMERICA

by Gerald B. Nelson

ISBN: 0-394-46610-1
Library of Congress Catalog Card Number: 72-171129

Grateful acknowledgment is extended to the following for permission to reprint excerpts from their works:

Djuna Barnes: From *Nightwood* by Djuna Barnes. Copyright 1936 by Faber and Faber, Ltd. (British edition), Copyright 1937 by Harcourt, Brace (U.S. edition).

Delacorte Press: From *God Bless You, Mr. Rosewater* by Kurt Vonnegut, Jr. Copyright © 1965 by Kurt Vonnegut, Jr. A Seymour Lawrence Book/Delacorte Press.

Farrar, Straus, & Giroux, Inc.: From *Wise Blood* by Flannery O'Connor. Copyright © 1949, 1952, 1962 by Flannery O'Connor. From *The Electric Kool Aid Acid Test* by Tom Wolfe. Copyright © 1968 by Tom Wolfe.

To Alix, and my daughters, Shawn and Corin

CONTENTS

PREFACE

Fear, frustration, and small stolen joys. All the roads lead either to death, oblivion, or the Land of Oz. Whom do we want to travel with—Humbert Humbert, Dick Diver, or Yossarian? Do we walk the road alone, or do we want an army? Ragged children—who commands them? What office? What building? Is Major Major in? And when it comes time to write the histories, who will be left to write them?

Once the land is gone, will we still have money?

Questions are no good. We already know the answers.

F. Scott Fitzgerald and Ernest Hemingway woke up in the Midwest and found themselves in America. They left.

"Goodbye, my fathers." Vladimir Nabokov left his rich beautiful language behind and fell into the cheap slang of upstate New York. Nathanael West went to Hollywood to write the words that go with moving pictures. Kurt Vonnegut won't write novels any more. Djuna Barnes sealed off a section of Greenwich Village so that the world would stop talking to her. Joseph Heller left advertising to discover money. Philip Roth's humor and hatred fought each other to the death. And Saul Bellow belongs to the Committee of Social Thought.

Back to the ground, damn you! Pick the green paper off it, and try to find some dirt! Tell your "different drummer" to play your own tune! Retch on mountain roads, but, please, keep your ears open, because children still live in the valleys. Don't let your existence be clubbed out of you in some drainage ditch somewhere. "There is no other city."

The American Dream has fulfilled itself. It is reality, dream no longer.

Mr. Sandman woke us up and spit gravel in our eyes. We blink and accept it.

Jonathan Edwards—how wrong you were! We're like spiders in the Eye of God, all right, but we made God. We cut down the trees for His temples and we poured the concrete for His shoes. We've pulled Him out of Heaven and tied Him to the land we claim is His. It is, but it was ours first, and we have made a very shoddy secondhand deal, cheating Him with some war-surplus merchandise. Rubber life rafts and fatigue jackets.

The Dream was the land. Room for everybody. But we had to own it. We do. Some of us. A lot more than some fell off the Great American Express train when it took the curves in the Rockies a bit too fast.

Brief Biographies:

Barnes, Jake. Wounded in the war. Impotent. Tried to keep the peace. Let others do what he wanted to, so long as they didn't hurt each other. Didn't understand human nature. A washerwoman.

Diver, Dick. Psychologist. "Lucky Dick." Married money. Liked "ickle durls." Looked into himself, discovered that maybe he could (did?) rape a five-year-old girl. Mistake. Fallen Puritan. Someplace in some small town in upstate New York.

Rosewater, Eliot. Millionaire. Rosewater Foundation. Bayoneted young volunteer fireman in the throat during the Second War. Crazy. Gave his money away to the poor for them to buy the crap the middle class worked to buy.

Lonelyhearts, Miss. Real name unknown. Wanted to help the suffering. Christ complex forced him to demand pain. Hated the touch of other human beings. Martyr's death.

O'Connor, Dr. Matthew. Unlicensed gynecologist. Transvestite. Saw and knew everything and everybody. Wanted to be left alone. Incorrigible drunk and garrulous public fool.

Motes, Hazel. Southern poor-white trash. Tried to escape Christ. Couldn't. Beaten to death by a cop. Died in a squad car.

Wilhelm, Tommy. Fortyish. Failure. Wants love. Needs money. Loses all, including self-respect, in the final day he must seize.

Klugman, Neil. Librarian. Puritan. Tries Short Hills. Fails. Will try again. Hates others and knows he's right. Will make it next time.

Yossarian. Paranoid. Knows that everyone is out to kill him. Is right. Jumps out of window. Now in Sweden, or Oz, or on the planet of Trafalmadore (if you believe in fairy tales). Anyway, he's alive. Not coming back.

Humbert, Humbert. Pervert. Lover. Believed in dreams; accepted and adored reality. Died in jail while awaiting sentence for the wrong crime.

Broken hearts. Wasted lives. Look at the water next time you go to the ocean; look for the great white dying body of Moby Dick and the dead beckoning hand of Ahab.

Jails, funny-farms, squad cars, stairways, funeral parlors. Why must we kill our saints in such ignominy?

I used to roll drunk Indians in Spokane, Washington. When they worked as gandy dancers for the railroad they usually had some change on Friday night. The government automated the railroads, and the only kicks I could get were in hurting the Indians, because they were out of work. Sad; the end of the joys of youth.

THE AMERICAN
GRAIN

To the Western World

A siren sang, and Europe turned away
From the high castle and the shepherd's crook.
Three caravels went sailing to Cathay
On the strange ocean, and the captains shook
Their banners out across the Mexique Bay.

And in our early days we did the same.
Remembering our fathers in their wreck

We crossed the sea from Palos where they came
And saw, enormous to the little deck,
A shore in silence waiting for a name.

The treasures of Cathay were never found.
In this America, this wilderness
Where the axe echoes with a lonely sound,
The generations labor to possess
And grave by grave we civilize the ground.

—LOUIS SIMPSON

William Carlos Williams:

And so they stressed the "spirit"—for what else
could they do?—and this spirit *is* an earthly pride which
they, prideless, referred to heaven and the next world.
And for *this* we praise them, instead of for the one thing
in them that was valuable: their tough littleness and
weight of many to carry through the cold; not their
brokenness but their projection of the great flower of
which they were the seed.

The Pilgrims were mistaken not in what they did, because they went hard to work with their hands and
heads, but in what they imagined for their warmth.

The Puritans put their hands to work on the land and
then lied to themselves because they felt that it was wrong
to say "This is for me," or, "I like what I have done."
Stupid, destructive selfishness, afraid to say its own name,
forced their eyes Heavenward, glazed over with the madness of good confused by guilt, of success swallowed by
impossibility. "Thank you, God. Whatever insignificant

4

joys I have achieved are due to You. My sorrows are my own."

If we think that we are now witnessing the failure of all that could have been America, we are wrong. It may be the failure of the dreams of Daniel Boone and others like him who went out and did honorable battle with the worlds they lived in.

But Boone's is not the spirit that emerged triumphant. He walked out into the wilderness and introduced himself, and if the bear refused his hand he tried to find out why, to make the hand, if not acceptable, at least recognized. He learned about things, not from guilt or malice but because he needed to, not to conquer but to live.

Jonathan Edwards tells his spider parable in spite of Ahab standing terrible and peg-legged screaming out his hate, and we listen as we always have and always will, because that is the song of America, the hymn we understand and have memorized in the very depths of our souls.

> Whole crisis of Christianity in America that the military heroes were on one side, and the unnamed saints on the other! Let the bugle blow. The death of America rides in on the smog. America—the land where a new kind of man was born from the idea that God was present in every man not only as compassion but as power, and so the country belonged to the people; for the will of the people—if the locks of their life could be given the art to turn—was then the will of God. Great and dangerous idea! If the locks did not turn, then the will of the people was the will of the Devil. Who by now could know where was what? Liars controlled the locks.

Norman Mailer, looking back at the flower armies facing the supreme bayonet of the Pentagon, is right, but he should have gone a little bit further. The idea of a country belonging to a people possessed of a power come from God is more than "great and dangerous"; it is terrifying.

Tom Wolfe recreates the end of the Acid Graduation: a scene between Ken Kesey and Ken Babbs:

> All the lights are out now, just a little glow from the dials of Prankster Control Center . . . Kesey and Babbs have their eyes closed, strumming slowly . . . alone in the center of the vast gloom of the bar. . . . The whole world contracts, draws closer and deeper and crawls inside the headsets, ricocheting in variable lag in the small hours, and Kesey sings over his guitar, which twangs and wobbles:
>
> ". . . and every now and then you can hear her blowing smoke rings around a cloud and trying to lace up her shoe . . ."
>
> And Babbs: ". . . and the message goes out and it breaks out just a little bit but—stops—"
>
> And Kesey: "It's kind of hard, playing cello on the hypodermic needle and using a petrified bat as a bow . . ."
>
> And Babbs: "Yes, it's hard working with these materials, without the grins falling off your knees . . ."
>
> And Kesey: ". . . and the soldiers think of the lowly fleas . . ."
>
> And— ". . . the latrines wade back up around my knees . . ."
>
> "So let's set here in this dilapidated people hutch and think about the things we've done . . ."
>
> ". . . Yes . . . down in Mississippi, that bitch girl we diddled in the cotton fields . . ."
>
> "Still . . . you want to catch the first subway to Heaven . . ."
>
> "If I can get myself a new set of scales, I'll get my ass off this third rail . . . and so saying, he stood up and

retched and looked down on the rail on sparks and long and hairy slavers of various flavors of dark intestinal brown . . ."

". . . and his teeth fell out by the dozen and Hitler and his infested cousins began to grow in the cellar like a new hybrid corn and the crows wouldn't touch him . . ."

". . . and up the rail, old True Blue wiped his nose on his uncle's clothes . . ."

"I took some pseulobin and one long diddle . . ."

"WE BLEW IT!"

". . . Ten thousand times or more . . ."

"WE BLEW IT!"

". . . so much we can't keep score . . ."

"WE BLEW IT!"

". . . Just when you're beginning to think, 'I'm going to score.' . . ."

"WE BLEW IT!"

". . . but there's more in store . . ."

"WE BLEW IT!"

". . . if we can get rid of these trading stamps that get in the way of the merchandise . . ."

"WE BLEW IT!"

". . . Ten million times or more! . . ."

"WE BLEW IT!"

". . . it was perfect, so what do you do? . . ."

"WE BLEW IT!"

". . . perfect! . . ."

"WE BLEW IT!"

Trading stamps, whether they be acid trips or fearful prayers to a God who already has his mind made up, do "get in the way of the merchandise." From the very beginning in America, the power and the glory has been translated into the coin of the realm, and if, at the time of the 1967 Pentagon March, "liars controlled the locks," who has ever accused Hooker, Mather, or Edwards of telling the truth? And if we stand astonished at the violence of our day, we need only remember that the "hard-hats" went to Merry Mount in 1627, filled with an insane envy that they could only translate into murder.

When, in *In the American Grain*, William Carlos Williams talks about the "spirit" in America, he talks about two spirits, contradictory, with one hateful and intolerable to the other. The first is the Puritan spirit:

> This [Merry Mount] in its simplicity the Puritans lacked spirit to explain. But spiritless, thus without grounds on which to rest their judgments of this world, fearing to touch its bounties, a fissure takes place for the natural mouth—and everything's perverse to them.

The second type of spirit Williams finds in Daniel Boone:

> Some one must have taken the step. He took it. Not that he settled Kentucky or made a path to the west, not that he defended, suffered, hated and fled, but because of a descent to the ground of his desire was Boone's life important and does it remain still loaded with power, —power to strengthen every form of energy that would be voluptuous, passionate, possessive in that place which he opened.

"Voluptuous, passionate, possessive." That means putting one's mouth to the earth, tasting it, relishing the animal in man that makes him human; it means being Arthur Dimmesdale and loving the fact. It does not mean the perfected callousness that turns Sister Carrie into a star with the broken, spat-upon wreckage of Hurstwood bobbing in her wake.

This spirit is as gentle as it is tough. When we read

8

books now, we see it in forms much different from the simple directness that Williams found in the life of Boone. Lewis and Clark won the West and the Boones now must wear disguises; so the spirit of the free jumps out the window with Yossarian, or gives its money away with Eliot Rosewater, or retches, cries and laughs on lonely mountain roads with Humbert Humbert. It is still alive but it cannot afford the time to sleep.

Williams called the Puritans "spiritless," but it wasn't lack of spirit that enabled them not only to survive but to conquer as well. It was what they did with the warped enormity of the spirit they possessed that created America. In the damp, cold darkness of New England nights, they forged the weapons that in time were to find a home in the massive anonymity of the Pentagon that so frightened Norman Mailer. Datta. Dayadhvam. Dhamyata. Give. Sympathize. Control. It was the third that the Puritans practiced and perfected. They learned to control the way an apprentice carpenter learns to use a hammer: by constant practice. They held their lives tightly—strengthened, not destroyed, by their fear. That the world was an enemy they knew; they had seen it many times, in England, in Holland, and now in a strange, uncharted new world, and they knew that if one were to deal with an enemy he needed weapons. And first among these had to be self-control.

They stood with their backs against the sea, with nothing but forests and strange red faces before them, and they must have wanted so terribly to simply go home again, but the gates had closed behind them. This now was home; it *would* be, no matter how hard "it" protested. So tighten up, get a hold on yourself! Walk into the God-damn wil-

9

derness and make it yours. Save "it" and yourself for God. But be wary, because it doesn't want to be saved; yet be strong because you're doing this incredibly frightening thing for God. This is what He wants you to do. So scared, homeless foreigners, carrying what had been their lives in little bags, walked out into the woods of the beautiful land that was to become their country, wanting, really, things only for themselves, but, knowing that that must be wrong, squinting their eyes shut against the beauty and screaming the Name of God in their minds.

That was self-control. Knowing that they were nothing, unwanted, unloved, and persecuted, they blessed an angry God for giving them a new hardship and dedicated the bounty of their new land to the spite of His terrifying Name. Williams again:

> In fear and without guidance, really lost in the world, it is they alone who would later, at Salem, have strayed so far—morbidly seeking the flame,—that terrifying unknown image to which, like savages, they too offered sacrifices of human flesh. It is just such emptiness, revulsion, terror in all ages, which in fire—a projection still of the truth—finds that which lost and desperate men have worshiped. And it is still to-day the Puritan who keeps his frightened grip upon the throat of the world lest it should prove him—empty.

Some fifty years later, in *The Armies of the Night*, Norman Mailer wrote, mixing newspaper reports and his own words:

> Troops, marching off the Mall after the anti-war crowd had been taken away, got a round of applause from their comrades on the line, the U.S. Marshals.
> Within 20 minutes after the jail-bound vans had

gone, two sweeper trucks had collected the debris left by the two-day campers—tomato juice cans, an empty bottle of expensive gin, a few tattered hippies' togas, stacks of paper and discarded magazines, a paperback entitled "Irrational Man," and assorted remnants of food. . . .

That same newspaper story had quoted a Pentagon spokesman's reaction to charges of brutality by Pentagon marchers: "We feel," said the spokesman, "our action is consistent with objectives of security and control faced with varying levels of dissent." . . .

A group from the Quaker Farm in Voluntown, Connecticut, practiced non-cooperation in prison. Among them were veterans of a sleep-in of twenty pacifists at the Pentagon in the spring before. Now, led by Gary Rader, Erica Enzer, Irene Johnson, and Suzanne Moore, some of them refused to eat or drink and were fed intravenously. Several men at the D.C. jail would not wear prison clothing. Stripped of their own, naked, they were thrown in the Hole. There they lived in cells so small that not all could lie down at once to sleep. For a day they lay naked on the floor, for many days naked with blankets and mattress on the floor. For many days they did not eat nor drink water. Dehydration brought them near to madness.

Dhamyata, "Our action is consistent with objectives of security and control." God is gone, but He is no longer needed; man can now hold man as he tries desperately to spin out his web-like hope, and laugh. We have walked away from Plymouth Rock, leaving it speckled with the dung of dead dreams, and built a better one. Peter, Plymouth, and Pentagon, they all begin with "P," and like Dr. Tamkin's "Four 'M's" (Money, Murder, Machinery, and Mischief), they represent a logical progression. Give a man a rock to cling to and, crab-like, he'll scurry under a bigger one, where he can dig himself a safer hole.

There were safe holes in the Massachusetts Bay Colony, but they were very small ones. Something like Morton's audacity at Merry Mount was to the Puritan Elders as terrible a reality as China was to William Knowland, a gasping for air that seemed to them a tumor on the delicate social organism that they, god-like, were constructing: cancerous, early-warning, it had to be cut out. It was.

In Salem. Moths to candle flames. Cotton Mather sat in the back row of an early-American 42nd Street movie house, with his hat on his lap, with the stern look of the really guilty on his face, with the power of fear in his hands, with the secret of lust in his heart, and, best of all, with the ability to destroy bursting throughout his entire being. He did. That is control. But something happened to the self. That scared nobody who first put his foot in the water off Plymouth Rock became somebody, and the God he used for security became a real and usable weapon. The power that Mailer talks about, that "great and dangerous idea," came to fruition very early in the infancy of this country; our first governors knew how to use it. They thought it; made it work; and they baptized it as the American Dream.

America is easily the most secular nation in history. Success is so easy here that we have made failure a sin. Money.

Poor Richard: Save, be rich—and do as you please— might have been his motto, with an addendum: provided your house has strong walls and thick shutters.

No one has ever accused Ben Franklin of being a fool.

Do something, anything, to keep the fingers busy—
not to realize—the lightning. Be industrious, let money
and comfort increase; money is like a bell that keeps the
dance from terrifying, as it would if it were silent and
we could hear the grunt,—thud—swish. It is small, hard;
it keeps the attention fixed so that the eyes shall not see.

Think of the dance that the Pilgrims found when they
entered the forests of the New World. It must have been
terrifying. They were tight unto themselves; each man
pulled into a knot, and the knots fashioned in an unbroken
circular rope. They knew nothing of the land, because they
had never known a place where they could touch it. They
knew only simple skills, things that they could do with their
hands to hide themselves. They were very frail, tiny, and so
scared that it is only their descendants who can damn them
by saying that they weren't. They built their little houses,
all clustered together, and worked and worked until they
were so exhausted that they would not have to lie sleepless
on their beds at night with the great throbbing heart of the
world they had stumbled onto beating horror into their
souls.

But they knew the heart was there, and that was the
terror in the dance. The forests fell before those small hands
with makeshift tools in them, and the creatures of the forest
ran, like Bambi, until they, too, found themselves with their
backs against an ocean, and the music of the dance was
stilled at last.

It was all done for God.

And then for Country.

And, finally, the dread whisper found breath: for Self.
Not malice, just fear. They couldn't look at the land

and say, "This is Mine," so they made it theirs by destroying it, by making it as unworthy in the Eye of God as they knew they were.

Money. William Carlos Williams hated Ben Franklin because he thought that Franklin was a con man, mouthing platitudes, making money, winking at God over the bowed heads of the world.

Yet what's the sense of having a God who doesn't understand you, and what, really, is the sense of living in a world that's better than you are? Franklin understood these things. He was maybe the first American who did and knew what to do with his understanding. We laugh fearful laughter at Joseph Heller's caricature of American Enterprise, Milo Minderbinder; but Milo is no other than Poor Richard in uniform, and if he couldn't manage to buy France, he surely would be our ambassador there.

In a land where dollar bills are served at communion breakfasts, the pimp must have a sense of humor. He must know he is lying. The taker is always in danger of being taken, and only hate, condescension, and guile save him. Yet the world must never know that it is hated. Tell a man that he can make a profit and he'll never check your bank account; Number One must always remember the other digits.

What is the American Dream, anyway? Williams looked for it all the way from Red Eric to Abraham Lincoln, "a woman in an old shawl—with a great bearded face and a towering black hat above it," giving "unearthly reality," and all he found were spirits. Varieties of fear, with different names. Call this one success; this one failure; but let there be no ink spots on the ledger. Saul Bellow's

Tommy Wilhelm was no accident. Williams saw him writ giant-size in Aaron Burr, and poor, incompetent Major Major is really just George Washington with his wooden teeth out.

We go and look at our monuments in this country; we stand at Hawthorne's desk and look at the new Piers moving relentlessly toward Portugal; we see Walden Pond through a bus window and stop to buy a hot dog; and we face the monuments at Concord and Lexington bravely and proudly. But our real glory is Mount Rushmore, where the magic of human ability and desperation has made the images of living Lilliputians survive time as still Brobdignagians chopped out of rock, wearing restaurants for hats. There we can worship—cold stone faces standing in dreadful Dakota isolation—without fear, because if such a thing as this is possible, then this land truly is our land, and only a new geologic period can inflict the fate of Shelley's Ozymandias upon us.

Maybe that's the Dream. Mount Rushmore was expensive, but then we haven't had a real bargain in this country since the Louisiana Purchase. We couldn't understand, much less love, the land, and so we set up idols, first God and then money. If we can really believe in the dollar, then we can name and carve mountains.

There used to be a phrase, "making a living." We've now dropped the "living" out of it and shortened it to simply "making It," and no one ever bothers to ask what "It" is. There is no need to; we all know already. God bless us.

Ahab, the crippled, angry bastard, yowled for his soul, but he captained a Quaker boat out of Nantucket, and there, souls had already been disposed of; the merchant had only his job left him. What was left for Ahab? The only things that he couldn't handle—the vast, cold sea and the whale, the white whale, in the imperfect whiteness of its body offering the real and terrifying temptation of murder and damnation. If there is no God, is there still a Satan? And from the beginning, who could tell the difference between them? Was there one? Answers. How this country needed them. But nobody dared ask the questions. So there was and is dullness and desperation; control and freedom, if one dare call fear by that name. Dimmesdale becomes Hurstwood becomes Jake Barnes, and Ahab, mute and terrified, becomes Dick Diver, going after the rotting whiteness of the whale in his own soul, and ends up drunk and impotent, giving away Princess telephones under the name of Eliot Rosewater, in a backwoods town in Indiana.

William Carlos Williams looked for the spirit in America, and now Norman Mailer prays for it.

Norman Mailer. America's clown. The fool from Tennyson's *Idylls of the King* telling his country that it will never laugh again. Camelot—but Arthur couldn't pull Excalibur from the stone, and all we can do is to name superhighways and airports after him, as we weep watching his barge float down polluted rivers. We have filled Old Faithful with so many beer cans that its timing is shot, and Norman Mailer asks us to pray:

> O Lord, forgive our people for they do not know, O Lord, find a little forgiveness for America in the puny reaches of our small suffering, O Lord, let these hours count on the scale as some small penance for the sins of

the nation, let this great nation crying in the flame of its own gangrene be absolved for one tithe of its great sins by the penance of these minutes, O Lord, bring more suffering upon me that the sins of our soldiers in Vietnam be not utterly unforgiven—they are too young to be damned forever.

The "toughness" is gone from that "littleness" for which Williams honored the Puritans, and it really does seem that we "are too young to be damned forever." Yet littleness and damnation walk hand in hand, and the elect of our country prefer it that way; they know no other.

The land! don't you feel it? Doesn't it make you want to go out and lift dead Indians tenderly from their graves, to steal from them—as if it must be clinging even to their corpses—some authenticity, that which—
Here not there.

Williams is talking about Quebec and Champlain and the French, but we can see the buying of Manhattan— marvelous bargain—or Franklin, in contrived shabby opulence, taking down the last dregs of a worn and dying France.

"The land! don't you feel it?" Americans crossed their land in heavy, hobnailed boots, better shod than their horses, and not even the fastest ants could get out of the way, and baby birds died in nests because the great thuds drove their mothers away.

No, William Carlos Williams, we don't "feel It." But you knew that, as have so many others. You have your dream of Boone, and we all share in the certainty of Thoreau, who did feel *it*—lonely, damned man, crawling around on his knees, rubbing his lovely, warm face in the incredible bounty he had discovered. And then he tried to talk about it.

Jacataqua, Sachem of the Indians of Swan Island, scares Williams. She says:

"These," with a wave of her brown hand toward Howard and the group of officers, "these want meat. You hunt with me? I win."

She was "scarce eighteen" when she said that to young Aaron Burr.

It is our need that is crying out, that and our immense wealth, the product of fear,—a torment to the spirit; we sell—but carefully—to seek blessings abroad. And this wealth, all that is not pure accident—is the growth of fear.

Burr wasn't frightened by the Indian girl, but she shook his training. She was more than beautiful; her beauty was her being. She looked at him with open eyes. "I win," and he knew that she would. What Williams saw in the Indians, and wanted to believe that Boone and Burr saw as well, was the directness of their lives. They did not have to approach life, because they were living it. They did not need our words, because their own meant things. What on earth could "make a living" mean to a man who was *living* with his people and the land? It is something that we cannot understand, because we try to. In a world where people put on masks to tantalize and then to frustrate others; where living means "making a killing" and that which is killed for is a dollar bill; where we need all our guile to hide our emptiness, and our lust is far more than we need and more than our neighbor has; where our bodies are dead and our minds frantic with fear—how, in a world like that, could we ever hope or want to know? "Our immense wealth, the product of fear."

Who is open to injuries? Not Americans. Get hurt; you're a fool. The only hero is he who is not hurt. We have no feelings for the tragic. Let the sucker who fails get his. What's tragic in that? That's funny! To hell with him. He didn't make good, that's all.

In America, people want to admire politicians. Not because they are the finest of the men among us, but because of the artistry of their skill in lying.

Jesus! It's no wonder that the pages of *In the American Grain* are filled with Williams's tears, or that Norman Mailer can describe America:

Brood on that country who expresses our will. She is America, once a beauty of magnificence unparalleled, now a beauty with a leprous skin. She is heavy with child—no one knows if legitimate—and languishes in a dungeon whose walls are never seen.

I don't think that the Puritans knew what they were doing. They wanted to hide, to protect themselves from the world, but not, surely, to burn down every tree, kill every animal, and leave their descendants with no more to do than overturn rocks so that they could crush insects. Not that. We who have come after them have done things with their fear that they could never have envisioned; taken their small spite and, spelling it "p-r-i-d-e," spread it giant and— Mailer's right—"leprous" over the land, until now some of us are terrified of trying to scratch the scab off, and others of us so horribly, totally dead from listening to our own lies that we'd like to rip it off just to watch the pus ooze out of the earth. And over all of us, gliding in giant, lazy circles in the air, are our leaders, the Elders of today, telling us that we don't need to touch, that if we just look at it as they do that we will find it beautiful, that "IT" is the real and the right world, and that we should be proud that we helped to make "IT" the way it is.

The reflecting pool is filled with Billy Graham's Murine and Daniel Boone commits suicide every hour on the half hour—admission $1.50, under 12 seventy-five cents—standing on top of the Golden Gate Bridge.

And where is Walt Whitman—that old pansy—going around and kissing young soldiers when they needed it. Laugh at him. But he really cried when Lincoln died. The queer tears of genius. Afraid of the dark.

Go to Salem sometime. It's always gray there—the sky, the land, and the faces of those who show you the relics in the houses of the people we killed for being witches.

And then go to Chicago.

Go with Norman Mailer:

> Yes, Chicago was a town where nobody could ever forget how the money was made. It was picked up from floors still slippery with blood, and if one did not protest and take a vow of vegetables, one knew at least that life was hard, life was in the flesh and in the massacre of the flesh—one breathed the last agonies of beasts. So something of the entrails and the secrets of the gut got into the faces of native Chicagoans. A great city, a strong city with faces tough as leather hide and pavement, it was also a city where the faces took on the broad beastiness of ears which were dull enough to ignore the bleat-

ings of the doomed, noses battered enough to smell no more the stench of every unhappy end, mouths—fat mouths or slit mouths—ready to taste the gravies which were the reward of every massacre, and eyes, simple pig eyes, which could look the pig truth in the face.

I lived there. I was there when John Kennedy was assassinated. I went to a bar and a guy was singing "Happy Days Are Here Again." He said, "We got him, now we'll get his brother."

We did. Pride. Group spirit.

Merry Mount. Communists. Indians. Beat, copping-out kids. We shot buffalo from train-car windows because we could do it and nobody else could, and it only made us angry for a little while when we discovered that there were none left.

It's our energy that's incredible. We are so scared that we can't stop, and the rubbish that we kick under picnic tables is not so much what we can't eat, but what we've never been able to feel.

"WE BLEW IT!"

But what the hell was "IT?" Running, our nervous systems gone forever, holding our fear over our heads like a shield. Why didn't we realize when we were doing "IT" that we were going to get caught?

Williams does.

He goes after the Puritans, because he was one. But instead of hiding, he tries to walk bareheaded and, with his surgeon's hands, to slice open his guilt. *In the American Grain* is a fearless, terrified book. It hurts to read it because Williams was a very brave man. He wanted to know what his land and his heritage were all about, and so he went out and joined them. He was born too late to be Thoreau, much less Boone, and he wanted to find out why. He did.

Williams does not observe; he lives along with the people he writes about. He really tells his own story. And if we listen, we will discover that it is our own as well.

It is the sad song of our country in our century. The sounded note that breaks our glasses: one chord of fear and remorse.

We know now what that white whale was and why Ahab had to try to kill it; we know what Dimmesdale felt; why Leatherstocking was really so detestable; and why Mark Twain had to hide Huck Finn in the tiny, nasty shadow of Tom Sawyer. Williams saw "IT" in the doomed, right defiance of Jacataqua; Mailer in the pale faces of the flower children and Guardsmen lined up facing each other in front of the final American building: the Pentagon. Others have seen "IT," too.

JAKE BARNES

Ernest Hemingway thought of American Literature as two ice-cream cones, little end to little end, with *Huckleberry Finn* in the middle siphoning in everything good and then passing it back out again, itself remaining inviolate, tidy, and perfect.

The American Dream is based upon the Puritan work ethic and the belief that there is room for everyone in an always expanding economy, that it is the fault of the individual if he doesn't succeed. A simple, direct, and economical approach to life. It meant that the "good" things in life are those obtainable through a directed, diligent, and sustained attack on the world around one. And any examination of the inner life is not only dangerous but sinful.

To be sick is to be sissy; à la Jake Barnes, man lives in the face of his troubles with grim, isolated determination. Good men die or are wounded terribly, but they can take it, and that's what makes them good. So Francis Macomber dies at his moment of truth and joins the sainted, and Frederic Henry learns the truth of man's loneliness and the importance of survival. These are honest, virtuous lessons and truths, American truths. Life, like any other game, can be won or lost. What is important is the way one plays it. None of this is original with Hemingway; it is the basic fabric of the American Dream. Success is possible in spite of circumstances if man has the right attitude, the healthy attitude.

What Scott Fitzgerald's Dr. Diver discovers, in *Tender Is the Night*, "Dr. Matthew-Mighty-grain-of-salt-Dante-O'Connor," in Djuna Barnes's *Nightwood*, knew all the time, Tommy Wilhelm, of Saul Bellow's *Seize the Day*, feels in his bones, and Nathanael West's Miss Lonelyhearts tries so painfully to escape. Diver wants to help, to bring the world back to sanity. He has sensitivity, he has beauty, he has training; he marries money. But Diver has too much, and he takes a chance that Jake Barnes never takes; he decides to look into himself. The Barnes approach to life is the unquestioning one, the basic assumption being that one must believe, at least, in oneself. You are—no matter what the rest of the world is or does—right.

The basic premise of this approach to life is "to thine

own self be true." But one must be careful never to look too closely at the self one is being true to, for it is not a "real" self. It represents for the individual a posture he affects before the world, including himself. Like an artist *manqué*, he must believe that his mask is his self.

This approach in literature looks out at the world and judges it. It is heroic in the purest sense, because it assumes the essential inviolability of the hero, his purity in relation to the world. Even if the world is not whole, he can at least make believe he is so. Odysseus does not cry, while Achilles does. Odysseus is a sane man in a world gone mad and he conquers it. Yossarian, in Joseph Heller's *Catch-22*, is a sane man in a world gone mad and it is all he can do to survive. All Odysseus wants is to get back to his family, all Penelope wants is to remain faithful, all Telemachus wants is to grow up; they all succeed. All Tommy Wilhelm wants is to know his real name; he fails miserably. *The Odyssey* sings the homely virtues and makes them heroic. Odysseus had a dream and achieved it through strength, cunning, and a single-minded devotion to purpose. He was a man any Puritan would have been proud to call Father.

Jake Barnes has no dream at all. He faces life like Odysseus, but with nowhere to go and no way of getting there. All that is left is the manner, none of the matter. Bravery becomes, with Hemingway, important purely for its own sake. Directionless, the brave man is brave because that is all there is. Even the simple goals of Odysseus are impossible to achieve, and what we have left from Odysseus' purposeful movement is the mere gossamer fabric of the dream; from a dynamic way of moving through life we have come to a static pose, from content to pure form.

But then, Jake Barnes is wounded. His impotence makes it impossible for him to *really* go anywhere; he realizes, as Flannery O'Connor's Hazel Motes says, that "there is no other city." As a result of this knowledge, he passes off as strength the particular brand of stoicism which he practices. If Daniel Boone had not been able to walk, he would have had an excuse to leave the wilderness alone. Cripples can beg away from confrontations without, one hopes, being ridiculed. Unlike poor foolish Robert Cohn, Jake Barnes at all costs avoids confrontations, his justification being that "things like that are bad form."

It is no accident that hunting, bullfights, and various other "moments of truth" are at the center of the action in Hemingway's books. A "moment of truth" is a moment in which one glimpses something about oneself in confrontation with another, and the natural reaction is destruction of the other. A strange corruption of the idea of heroic nature and moments that began so long ago with Odysseus. Not that Odysseus was introspective. Thought was the very nature of his being. But when he addressed himself, it was in the "be brave, my heart" manner. What Odysseus did was to focus his reason on situations, to think first and act later. The Hemingway hero, if he thinks, does not act; if he acts, he does not think.

Odysseus believed that he was smart enough to—with Athena's help—remake the world. The Hemingway hero feels that he's smart, too, but that the smart thing to do is to leave the world alone, make it come to you if anybody's going anywhere. It won't. Impasse.

There is no attempt at positive movement toward something, either a person or an idea. This static pose is a defensive maneuver, intended to keep people and things out. Man refuses to examine himself or his motives, because what he has seems to work well enough. At least he is alive.

In literature this leads to boredom; in life it leads to the most grisly kind of suicide, a gradual withering away with a death mask of a smile on the face. How did we get here, from Odysseus to Jake Barnes? And why?

The First World War showed twentieth-century young men many things, opening their eyes to both their world and themselves. First, the romance of war and the *"dulce et decorum"* notion of serving one's country were shown to be complete and horrible nonsense. The war was ugly, filthy, brutal, and, above all, totally futile. Mired in trenches, men died and then rotted namelessly and facelessly. And these men were the young, the flower and hope of their countries. Others watched as the brilliant and the beautiful died around them, and it is no wonder that the living wondered why. The answer? So that the system may survive. Words of praise for their noble efforts reached them from home, and it seemed to them that only they knew that what they were doing was neither noble nor even decent. Moreover, they gradually realized that those same people who were praising them were getting fat off the war. The longer it lasted, with more of them dying, the more the money to be made at home. So the glory of battle, if there ever was such a thing, was nonexistent to them, as they fought and killed and were killed by an enemy they couldn't even see, and the cause of war, the virtue behind the fight, the reason for the death, was corrupt.

When the war finally ended and those who survived returned home, they were expected to apply gratefully for readmission into the system. They were heroes, but that was over now, and they were no different from anyone else, just a little older and a little behind. Some of them complied, taking jobs, returning to school. Others dropped out, either unwilling or unable to rejoin the system.

All over the world after the war, one found the disenfranchised and the disenchanted, English, American, French, and German, wandering their different ways, occasionally crossing paths, sharing a common motivation—the world they wanted was a different one from the one in which they were supposed to live. There had always been wanderers in Europe, but these particular ones were on the road because they wanted to be; they were escaping a totally new type of oppression. They just didn't like where they'd been; they could have stayed, but they didn't want to.

America had always been the place people went, not the place they left, especially not dissatisfied. The whole idea behind the American Dream was that there was room to do anything you wanted anywhere you wanted. If you didn't do it, it was nobody's fault but your own.

Some Americans, their eyes just opened to Europe by the newly discovered ease of travel (for that we have to credit the war), simply wanted to visit. Others, wealthy, suffered from a feeling of cultural lag, and wished to try out their carefully purchased French on the museum guards of Europe. But there were others who did not wish to go to Europe as much as they wanted to get out of the United States.

Jake Barnes

. . .

There is a certain wild, gutsy joy to the struggles and triumphs of Odysseus, because one knows that to the Greeks
life was all man had; once you die, it's over—there's nothing left but shadows. But America is a Christian country—
more properly, a Puritan one—and the things that one does
in it are done, at least in theory, with one eye on Heaven.
The joy of triumph here is diluted, as is the agony of failure. Man's works are important, but he is supposed to fool
himself into believing that what he does, he does in the hope
of an afterlife. So we talk about God while we try to make
money. This brand of hypocrisy works very well in a carefully structured and controlled society. You take bread,
give them God. But when you couple religious hypocrisy
to the other basic element of the American Dream, that it is
possible to develop and maintain a middle-class world with
freedom to make more money but, hopefully, never less,
you get into trouble. For those who already have things, an
ennui, a boring sameness of power takes over, and there
seems to be no place to go, no real reason for going there. It
was this ennui that effected the exodus of bright, would-be
creative, upper-middle-class WASPS from the United States
to Europe after the First World War.

Unlike the culture-hungerers, they were sincere. They
wanted to find a place where they could exist, if not work,
with honesty. Yet they were strange fish, for they brought
with them their own versions of the peculiar Puritan American vitality to a world where it just wouldn't work. They
had left home and said, sincerely, that they never wanted to
go back. But they missed it. They simply could not hon-

estly, permanently settle because no place was America. So they felt forced to construct little portable worlds they could carry about with them. These were conglomerates, mixed bags of French, English, German, Italian, and American, but the driving force in each of these miniature traveling societies, at least to the Americans who wrote about them, was American. It was quite natural that it should be. The American ego is quite different from that of any other nation. It is one American product that is not exportable. The American hopes to hell he's right and even if he isn't he will triumph. But there's no surety in him; centuries have not proved him right; he feels and is—to his own disgust, more than anyone else's—*nouveau riche*, and not only in dollars but in soul as well. The desperation we encounter in the portraits of Americans by Americans in book after book following the exodus of the literati after the First World War takes its root in the fear that the rest of the world will discover what they already know about themselves: that they are phonies. There is no more of Ben Franklin's pride or of Tom Paine's brashness. Just fear, and violent, pathetic attempts to get rid of the money that got them their villas to begin with.

They were new conquerors of their own land, and they brought with them to Europe a variation of the same attitude that had enabled their parents and grandparents to take a continent away from its inhabitants and then to try to pretend that it was really theirs. Wherever he goes, whether he knows it or not, the American comes, in general, not to assimilate, but to control. This is not malicious, it is nature. Yet moving in on a nation or nations that were nations with the history, government, and sophistication that historical stability brings with it was a far cry from moving in on a continent of disjointed, unsophisticated, semi-nomadic tribes. They simply could not take over, nor could they assimilate. That ran against the grain. So they set up their separate societies and moved from spot to spot, picking up the fringe members of various nations along the way. They became tourists of the most sincere and the most decadent sort simultaneously.

These are the people Hemingway and Fitzgerald wrote about. Their portraits of the disenchanted wanderers of other nations are naïve and condescending at best, malicious at worst. But their Americans show as complete a picture as one could wish of the two directions in approaching life that Americans were choosing between in the years following the Great War: between Franklin and Boone.

When Dick Diver, Rosemary Hoyt, and Abe North visit the sprawling war cemetery and encounter the weeping girl looking for her brother's grave amidst the endless fields of unmarked white crosses, we realize what one of those choices means. The girl cannot find the grave and Dick counsels her to place her bouquet on any grave, telling her that her brother would have wanted it that way.

When Priam went to Achilles and humbled himself by kissing the hand of the man who killed his son, he pointed out graphically just exactly how important life and death should be to an individual. To the Greek, death marked the end of an individual life and it had to be celebrated in an individual way: leaving a corpse, particularly a hero's corpse, for the carrion and dogs to feed on not only dishonored the man; it prevented his life from ending, his "shade" from being freed. So it was worth the worst sort of humiliation to Priam to recover Hector's body and pay his life its final proper respects: a hero's life and a hero's death. Death was looked upon as the fulfillment of a person's individuality and, at its occasion, a man was so treated.

That field of nameless white crosses put the final lie to Priam's plea. Put the flowers anywhere, it really doesn't matter. But if "It" doesn't, what does? Man has the quirk of ego that enables him to feel that he is important outside of himself, that he matters to others. We feel that, save in fits of madness, we act always with at least one eye on the world outside us. But if man begins to believe that his stature in the world is not what he felt it to be, that his death is not only meaningless but faceless as well, what does he then think about his life?

Jake Barnes and Dick Diver are children of America. For Jake Barnes, the fact of death is rendered totally unheroic, showing up as meaningless illusions all that he had felt to be his achievements as he dropped suddenly into oblivion. As with death, so with life. Jake Barnes approached life not with hope but with resignation. It was foolish to make plans, for the future was just as bleak and meaningless as the past, if, indeed, there was a future. Man existed in the present, taking, stoically, whatever pleasures existed in the moment. Joy would hurt, if not destroy, the pose. The idea of being a hero had descended to the notion of acting the part of being "one's own man," relatively safe from pain because relatively inured to pleasure. Jake Barnes, like all others of his ilk, exists in limbo; denied the life of the Greek, he denies himself the Heaven of the Christian. Barnes lives in a hedonistic world, yet he is wounded and unable to abandon himself to the pleasures around him. A steer among bulls by fate.

One cannot imagine that he would want it any other way.

He shows us, by example, inadvertent or not, the way to live. Aloof, taking what you can, always aware of your limitations and aware of those of your fellows as well, you tiptoe through the world, making believe you enjoy it. You're aware of your own impotence, of course, but after all it's better than being like those around you; at least it stops you from making a fool of yourself. So the moments Jake Barnes seizes are peculiarly his own, selected and savored in a carefully detached way.

But they mean something.

Barnes and *The Sun Also Rises* represent one approach that an individual could take to the "new" world that Americans felt themselves in after World War I. In this approach, one, like T. S. Eliot's Tiresias in *The Waste Land*, shores up fragments against his ruin, careful never to shatter his belief in himself. It is no wonder that Hemingway could never be imitated well, and it is no wonder that those who did the best job of it were writers like Mickey Spillane, who created fantasy worlds where a super-hero with a gun could wander cynically toward no discernible goal save brutality. Both the world and the hero are inhuman, simplistically so. One cannot, unless he is insane, isolate himself in a universe of his own creation, behind a mask he wishes were his face.

Jake Barnes believes that there is nothing that he can do. He loves Brett desperately, and also Bill, Mike, and even

Harris. He also cries over the impossibility of his love for Brett, and for the fate and foolishness of his friends: the ruined drunkenness of Mike and the boorishness of Cohn. He prays, not really knowing why, but because, for some reason or other, being a Catholic makes being easier. And he is truly at home in nature: trout-fishing outside Burguete with Bill, he is acutely aware of everything around him; every sense is active.

But for Jake Barnes everything passes, and he is aware at every moment that this is so. He knows that it is his responsibility to conceal this knowledge from those around him. Like a priest, he can absolve, but never dare to tell the truth. He tries to protect his flock, watching over them to prevent early deaths, because they want to stay alive, but he himself knows that there is no meaning in life, save that it is built on pain. Jake should see himself as a worldly-wise social director at a resort hotel, trying to keep the guests from getting into fights that are too dangerous, preserving the sad creatures so that they might go on to live another day: "a steer among bulls."

That is why Robert Cohn calls him a pimp, and why Jake gets so angry when Cohn does. He is a pimp. Not the self-aggrandizing, back-of-the-hand-to-the-cheating-whore type of pimp, but a pimp nonetheless. He pimps for the only person he really loves: Lady Brett Ashley—introducing her to men, covering for her when she disappears with them, and going to pick her up when she is through with them. Yet he gets no money for his labors, nor is he vicariously enjoying himself. Everything that Jake does in terms of Brett is done because he loves her.

To Jake Barnes, nothing is worse than being in bed at

night, the ultimate loneliness—any sober night in bed is a version of a "dark night of the soul." So Jake is better off drunk, or dulled, which passes as drunkenness for Jake, or with Bill; anything but alone.

By the time we meet Jake, he has assumed a mask of stoicism, so that he can comment on the world he sees and only cry silently at night in the isolation of his room. The public howl of anguish has long since stopped echoing. Everyone knows what happened to him, and it is no longer a subject of conversation. But the fact that Jake knows that everyone *knows* underlines his every comment and his every action. In a world dominated, however understated, by sex and violence, Jake is not only safe, he is essential. That is why everyone is so upset by Cohn's physical attack on Jake. Unable to take part in the action himself, he is needed as a buffer. He may be a pimp, but in the world through which the characters of *The Sun Also Rises* travel, a pimp is necessary. Without one, people would start killing each other as they do bulls, and as Cohn, with Jake out of the way, almost does Romero. Jake knows what he must do and he does it. He is the voice of conscience, advising, saying over and over: "I can't and you can, but please be careful. Try not to hurt anyone else."

It is a saintly role to play in life, and, like all saints, Jake Barnes hates it. It is not enough for him to have "afición"; he would like to have it fulfilled.

But that cannot be, and so he staggers though life, an unwilling priest, taking confession and, like a Miss Lonelyhearts with a sick, deadening self-control, watching his urge to love turn into a need to hate. Barnes knows his world and he thinks he knows his place in it. He knows that he is superior to those around him, and that they are dependent upon him to "keep the peace," but what he never learns, and only maybe glimpses in "l'affaire Cohn," is that he is wrong. He is not really needed by his friends; Breughel-like, blinder than all, he leads the blind, and leads them into more trouble than they could ever dream of finding by themselves. They are together only because he is there.

There were two answers for Jake: stay out of it, or commit suicide. So he does not choose. He stays in it, arranging rooms for everybody, taking people for drinks so that they will keep out of other people's business, literally walking the dog and doing the dishes for the world. While the world pretends gratitude for it, and is kind to the cripple.

Robert Cohn, fool and boor that he is, mixes it up with life. He throws punches—maybe the wrong ones, but at least he throws them. Of course, Cohn is stupid: a naïve, battered Jew, while Jake has no naïveté left, if he had any to begin with. Yet Robert Cohn's weakness is child-like in its innocence: his ego, if uncontrolled, is really harmless. He blunders through his life, like a bull with blinders on, believing in love, himself, and strangely enough, others— wanting friends, believing he has them, basically only wanting to shake hands after he makes a mistake, saying, "I'm sorry, I didn't know." A dummy; a loser; a Tommy Wilhelm with a better body.

Cohn, awkwardly, does what he sets out to do: laying Brett, beating up Romero, calling Jake a pimp. Jake thinks about things, about what might have been. But he really prefers self-pity as much as, if not more than, does Cohn; what happens to Cohn is, in Jake's eyes, his own fault, but what happened to Jake was a damned metaphysical joke. He had done nothing to deserve it. Maybe so, but what right does Jake have to be disgusted by Cohn's tears when he relishes his own so much? When Cohn pities himself, it is because he has acted badly, not because he has done nothing at all.

The Sun Also Rises is a rootless novel. There is no terrain in it. Paris does not necessarily have to be Paris. London or Rome would have done as well. Even Spain does not have to be Spain. A Forest Hills tennis tournament could easily replace the bullfights. One could not, for instance, imagine Miss Lonelyhearts playing out the horrible drama of his life in any darkness other than that of the New York City night, but Jake, Brett, and the others could be anywhere; their agonies have nothing to do with where they are. They compose a tight, microcosmic psychic universe of their own. They live in a deliberate limbo.

It's the fact that environment has no effect on the characters that gives *The Sun Also Rises* its overwhelming feeling of futility. There is no hope of moving. When Cohn suggests to Jake that they go to South America, Jake says, "All countries look just like the moving pictures"; and, later on in the same conversation,

> "Listen, Robert, going to another country doesn't make any difference. I've tried all that. You can't get away from yourself by moving from one place to another. There's nothing to that."

Humbert Humbert drives over and over America. And the Merry Pranksters blow their minds away on the sounds inside their Day-Glo bus.

The whole idea of the book is to keep away from yourself, and to help others by allowing them to suffer in the depths of their agonies by themselves, simply skimming surface troubles off like cream. There is a code in *The Sun Also Rises:* it goes something like this—"Keep away from other people if possible; if it isn't, then barely touch them, and if, by accident, you go too deeply into them and find something, keep your mouth shut." Cohn breaks the code. He constantly makes a public show of his emotions and embarrasses those around him with his honesty, finally even Jake. "You ain't true."

Of course, Cohn isn't meant to be the hero of *The Sun Also Rises*; that's Jake's role. The book opens with this sentence: "Robert Cohn was once middleweight boxing champion of Princeton." It is Cohn who causes the characters' concern: Is he coming? When? How long is he staying? How can we get rid of him? Like kids trying to ditch the unwelcome tag-along at the movies, they are constantly looking over their shoulders to see where Cohn is.

Cohn irritates by his activity, and by his unwillingness or inability to accept the tacit understanding that everyone else is to be left alone. He refuses to believe that cripples cannot be healed; that the only humane thing is to allow them to play out their lives in whatever fashion they are able to without trying to save them. Cohn is a misplaced knight, with a very confused notion of the courtly love tradition. He would like to slay a dragon for the honor of his lady, but his Lady Brett is, in fact, the very dragon herself; Romero does not violate her purity, and Jake is not an evil magician holding her under a spell. Yet, to Cohn's code of honor, that is how they appear. He loves Brett, so he must defend her against the forces of evil. The confused horror of Cohn's final actions: after knocking down both Jake and Mike, he goes to Romero's room!

"It seems the bull-fighter fellow was sitting on the bed. He'd been knocked down about fifteen times, and he wanted to fight some more. Brett held him and wouldn't let him get up. He was weak, but Brett couldn't hold him, and he got up. Then Cohn said he wouldn't hit him again. Said he couldn't do it. Said it would be wicked. So the bull-fighter chap sort of rather staggered over to him. Cohn went back against the wall.

" 'So you won't hit me? '

" 'No,' said Cohn. 'I'd be ashamed to.'

"So the bull-fighter fellow hit him just as hard as he could in the face, and then sat down on the floor. He couldn't get up, Brett said. Cohn wanted to pick him up and carry him to the bed. He said if Cohn helped him he'd kill him, and he'd kill him anyway this morning if Cohn wasn't out of town. Cohn was crying, and Brett had told him off, and he wanted to shake hands. I've told you that before."

"Tell the rest," Bill said.

"It seems the bull-fighter chap was sitting on the floor. He was waiting to get strength enough to get up and hit Cohn again. Brett wasn't having any shaking hands, and Cohn was crying and telling her how much he loved her, and she was telling him not to be a ruddy ass. Then Cohn leaned down to shake hands with the bull-fighter fellow. No hard feelings, you know. All for forgiveness. And the bull-fighter chap hit him in the face again."

"That's quite a kid," Bill said.

"He ruined Cohn," Mike said. "You know I don't think Cohn will ever want to knock people about again."

A Jew from Princeton, with his medieval code of honor all confused with the Marquis of Queensbury rules, Cohn

can, at the end, only try to shake hands; "No hard feelings," save for his own.

We are finally asked to choose: the "ruddy ass" or the
"steer among bulls"? Does it really make any difference? In
a world like that of *The Sun Also Rises*, Robert Cohns cannot exist, but is the existence of the Jake Barneses any the
more real because of that fact? Cohn is madly futile, trying
to make dreams reality in a society where the nightmare is
the accepted norm, and Jake is sanely impotent, trying to
exert just enough control to prevent disaster in a world that
is already dead. There is no real choice between the two
men, the one with his pathetically public tears and the other
sobbing alone in the dark of his room. Nor is there choice
between the two "ways," because the end for each is failure
and despair, whether public or private. Cohn trying vainly
to shake hands, Jake feeling Brett's body against him in the
taxi: it is all one and the same.

"Isn't it pretty to think so?"

DICK DIVER

Let's begin at the beginning.

On the pleasant shore of the French Riviera, about half way between Marseilles and the Italian border, stands a large, proud, rose-colored hotel. Deferential palms cool its flushed façade, and before it stretches a short dazzling beach. Lately it has become a summer resort of notable and fashionable people: a decade ago it was almost deserted after its English clientele went north in April. Now, many bungalows cluster near it, but when this story begins only the cupolas of a dozen old villas rotted like water lilies among the massed pines between Gausse's Hôtel des Étrangers and Cannes, five miles away.

No character appears, just a place. A particular place at a particular point in time approached in a particular manner.

We have a distance shot: an airplane coming down over an area, seeing at first over a distance of five miles (from Gausse's hotel to Cannes), finally focusing on the "short, dazzling beach." We see a panorama and we see it in the perspective of two periods of time, what it was and what it is, and then we are taken down still further, to the microscopic world of the beach, the world which is Dick Diver's when we first meet him. Dominated by the "hotel for strangers," deserted with the departure of the English for the North, save for its rotting villas and the people who inhabit them.

Jake Barnes did not want to settle; he had no desire to establish any world he could not carry in a suitcase or discard as he wished. Dick Diver was a settler. He wanted a home and he wanted a kingdom as well. So Diver settled in that world we encounter in the first paragraph of *Tender Is the Night,* taking the beach as his own special fief, hoping, vainly, that with control there, he would be safe.

We don't have Dick yet, just his world, and we meet the residents before we meet the king. First Abe North, floundering through his morning swim; then Rosemary Hoyt ("almost eighteen, nearly complete, but the dew was still on her") and her mother; then the British nannies and the dozen couples under their dozen umbrellas with their dozen children. All of these nameless at the start. Then, when Rosemary is identified, a flood of names begins; Campion, Mrs. Abrams, Mrs. McKisco, Mr. McKisco, Mr. Dumphry—but not the name of the "fine man in a jockey cap and red-striped tights" or those of the members of his party.

Fitzgerald is very careful in introducing us to Dick Diver's world. We meet people by their physical characteristics ("the hairy man"), or their dress ("the young woman with the string of pearls"), not by what they are or think. Diver, as we first see him, unnamed, is "giving a quiet little performance" with a rake. Rosemary Hoyt, the first character to be identified by both name and career, is a movie actress, and Violet McKisco, "a shabby-eyed, pretty young woman with a disheartening intensity," views the Divers and their friends as having a "plot," with Dick as hero and Abe North as assistant hero, at least "practically" so.

The feeling one has in reading the first few pages of *Tender Is the Night* is akin to that which one has in watching the beginning of a movie: all the things, people, and attitudes—in fact, all the "stuff" of the novel is before us and we see it. We don't understand it yet. The petty, desperate jealousy of the McKiscos, et al., we later find— magnified, but the same emotion—in the blind, supercilious superiority of Mary Minghetti (formerly North), Lady Caroline Sibly-Biers, and the impossible social-consciousness of Baby Warren. Nicole's face, "hard and lovely and pitiful," holds even at this early point the "crook's eyes." And Diver's "performance" with the rake, which is hilarious to everyone save Nicole, reverberates in his final drunken blessing of the beach.

In *The Sun Also Rises*, we know all we are going to

know about Jake Barnes the minute he opens his mouth. The interest is in his world and what we can discover about it. We don't need to know anybody, because nobody is really knowable.

In *Tender Is the Night*, we see the world first if not through at least with the virginal eyes of Rosemary Hoyt. We along with Rosemary want to be deflowered, and it is always a man, not a world, who does that. Hemingway had Jake Barnes tell us who he was and why he was the way he was in order to convince us of the efficacy of Barnes's position. Fitzgerald gives us nothing about Diver, save for a kind of glamorous feeling for his magnetism, because *Tender Is the Night* is about Diver, as *The Sun Also Rises* is not about Jake Barnes. *Tender Is the Night* is a voyage book. Not a voyage book like *The Odyssey*, where the courage, integrity, and intelligence of Odysseus are given and we only watch for their tests and triumphs, but a voyage-into-night book, like *Moby Dick*, where there are no givens, because the territory the man is traveling is the land of his own insides, and there is no map for it, and no sane attitude one could assume in approaching it. With Odysseus, success was certain. With Diver, we know and he knows that a successful journey brings with it horror. Like Oedipus, Diver learns that the fault is his and is therefore unconquerable, the sickness his and incurable. Odysseus reclaimed land and family; Jake Barnes realized that the only land and family he could claim was lodged within his own body and so he held on to it. Oedipus had everything, so did Dick Diver; they gambled it because they wanted to find out who they were, and when they found out, the

48

horror of it sent them into exile. It is the fall of pride that is so magnificent in an Oedipus or a Dick Diver, the success of it that is so stunning about Odysseus, the maintenance of it that is so incredible about a Jake Barnes. And the horror belongs to Ahab. Let him have at least that.

We do not know much about Dick Diver at the first. We don't know the image of the man to himself. We know only what he looks like, and that something about him not only amuses others, but seems to dominate them as well. His world seems a fantastic movie setting for a portrait of the decay of the once rich and worldly, brought about by the intrusion of the jealous bourgeois would-be intellectuals.

By the end of Chapter I, we have met the "gallery," as Mrs. Abrams refers to her group. Chapter II introduces us to the "cast." The gallery members envy the Divers their manner, the style and pattern of their behavior. To the outsiders, the insiders are not merely actors, but bad actors. Abe North, for instance, may be a good swimmer, but he's a "bad musician." If the judgment of Mrs. Abrams or the McKiscos is no more than nastiness, what they see is what we are meant to see as well. The Divers *are* presenting a play on the beach, but not for the amusement or displeasure of any outsiders. The purpose of the play is to keep them from looking inside themselves, to keep things running with the illusion of happiness. What so infuriates the McKiscos is that they believe the play is real, that the Divers and their friends are happy in a beautiful way, a way that makes them feel small, ugly, and inferior. Merry Mount. Fitzgerald, in showing us the reaction of the McKiscos before explaining what is really happening and who the participants are, is asking us not to be suckered into believing that what we see is all there is. He wants us to see it, but to know that there is more to what we see than mere manner.

When Rosemary walks out on the veranda of the hotel, it is "too bright to see," everything is bathed in "brutal sunshine," and "only the beach stirred with activity." We are meant to see this "activity" with all shadows stripped away or, at least, hidden.

Abe North is introduced not by name but as "the man with the leonine head," whose swimming ability is in marked contrast to McKisco's ineptitude and inability to breathe in the water. Then, as North surfaces under one of the two children playing in the water, "the woman of the pearls" is identified.

She is not North's wife; she is "Mrs. Diver. They're not at the hotel." Sickened by the McKiscos' pettiness, Rosemary swims back to shore, where she falls asleep in the sun, feeling that there is no life anywhere save under the umbrellas of the Divers, and "that it all came from the man in the jockey cap." When she awakes, she meets him. But not by name. Diver does not introduce himself, merely says, "It's not good to get too burned right away." He seems to possess a perfect self-composure, so that Rosemary feels able to live in the "bright blue worlds of his eyes, eagerly and confidently." Yet he does say one curious thing. When Rosemary asks the time and Dick tells her that it's one-thirty, he says, "It's not a bad time. It's not one of the worst times of the day."

What Diver means is that he knows the "worst times." We are not prepared by anything that has gone before in the glittering sunshine of the beach morning, or in the mindless malice of the McKiscos, for anything to do with darkness. And that is precisely what Diver offers up.

The sunshine of the first two chapters of *Tender Is the Night* is as false as the light of the klieg lights that Rosemary Hoyt encountered in the filming of *Daddy's Girl*. It is the false brilliance of Diver that so captivates her, that enables her to say, after one brief encounter on the beach, that she has fallen in love. The real stuff of the book is not this Hollywood sunlight, but the darkness of the night. Rosemary Hoyt is a naïf: like Dolores Haze with her movie madness, she wanders into Hell and mistakes it for Paradise.

It is easy to say, "Hell is other people." F. Scott Fitzgerald's Dick Diver would say, "Hell is me!" If one can say that Hell is other people and believe it, one can laugh. The individual is off the hook; his agony comes from without, not within. But if one believes that he himself is Hell, there is no escape; there is only one road and that leads straight within.

Dick Diver says (closing Book II), "I want to make a speech. I want to explain to these people how I raped a five-year-old girl. Maybe I did—"

He did. As surely as Mr. Warren turned his daughter Nicole, briefly, horrifyingly, into his lover. In his mind, Dick Diver knows that he likes "ickle durls." He knows that, despite his protestations of being a doctor with a patient, he married Nicole because she was young, and that his sweet, fatherly protective attitude toward Rosemary is neither sweet nor protective. The real reason that Diver fails as a psychoanalyst is not that he sells himself out to the Warren money (they did not, as Baby Warren liked to think, "buy themselves a doctor"), but that he looks into himself, and the healer, finding himself unhealable, finds it impossible to be a fraud. And the façade concealing the Divers' real life that the McKiscos find so detestable and Rosemary so irresistible, which insiders feel is there for the protection of Nicole, is really, as Tommy Barban, the single-minded mercenary, discovers, Dick's shield and only hope of protection from himself.

The journey into oneself is lonely, frightening, and, perhaps worst of all, unending. Diver doesn't die, he just slips out of sight, reduced by the end of the book from the seeming king of a miniature kingdom to an ever-shrinking speck on the map of the state of New York. ("In any case he is almost certainly in that section of the country, in one town or another.")

The confrontation of the self, not the mirror image, but the real self, and the simple statement, *"Mea culpa,"* or, as Diver would put it, "Maybe I did."

In the summer father and son walked downtown together to have their shoes shined—Dick in his starched duck sailor suit, his father always in beautifully cut clerical clothes—and the father was very proud of his handsome little boy. He told Dick all he knew about life, not much but most of it true, simple things, matters of behavior that came within his clergyman's range. "Once in a strange town when I was first ordained, I went into a crowded room and was confused as to who was my hostess. Several people I knew came toward me, but I disregarded them because I had seen a gray-haired woman sitting by a window far across the room. I went over to her and introduced myself. After that I made many friends in that town."

His father and his fathers before him possessed, as Diver was to think at his father's grave, "souls made of new earth in the forest-heavy darkness of the seventeenth century." The old darkness. The darkness of fear of the world outside, the world that man was gradually discovering was larger and more complex than either he or his God could handle. The faith that molded Diver's forefathers was a faith of desperation, shoring up God's might against the size of the universe. The founding faith of America. When Diver says, "Good-by, my father—good-by, all my fathers," he is doing much more than merely paying graveside obeisance to the dead. He is paying his respects to the decency of his father and ancestors as human beings, but he is also saying that their darkness is not his own, that he has gone across the room to introduce himself to the gray-haired lady and that it has not been enough, or simply not the right thing to do. He has not "made many friends in that town." The reaction of the ancestors of Diver to the darkness of the seventeenth century was a social one. The darkness was outside and people could band together, under God, to protect themselves from it; Dick Diver's twentieth-century darkness comes from within, and there is no way for another to come near it, much less protect him from it. There is no longer safety in numbers.

What Diver's father could offer him ("all he knew about life") was advice about "matters of behavior," how to act toward others, how to be nice, but he could offer him nothing in terms of dealing with himself, for to the clergyman that was forbidden territory. To his father and the entire fabric of the "healthy" American approach to life, Dick owes the ability to put on the show we encounter at the opening of the book, maintaining the illusion that all is not only well but better than ever, while his world is no more than an empty shell, or, as he says to Rosemary, "The change came a long way back—but at first it didn't show. The manner remains intact for some time after the morale cracks."

Diver, as are all Puritans, is set completely on his own when examining himself and as a consequence, borrowing Nicole's words, becomes a "mad Puritan." There is no choice for Diver. It may very well be that it is better to be a "sane crook" like Tommy Barban or Nicole, but, given himself to work with, Diver did the bravest and the only thing he could.

The key to understanding Diver lies in the "matters of behavior" that his father advised him about. This advice, which both Diver and Fitzgerald considered to be "all he knew about life," had to do only with manner, with how one looked to others, one's façade. To Diver's father, that was what was most important in life. And why not? Morals were taken care of by Christianity; one didn't do bad things, because they went against God's dictates. All that was left was to look and be nice.

Diver's father still believed in society. Fear motivated him as surely as it motivated Jake Barnes. It's just that he didn't know its name. His fear was assuaged by the belief in Divine salvation so long as he did his job on earth, while Barnes controlled his by believing in his own image of himself. It is this that makes them what Nicole might call "sane Puritans." They survive because they are not concerned, or at least will not admit to themselves that they could be, with real problems of self. For different reasons, they feel that there is nothing to be done about the way they are, and, contented or not, they ooze unreflective egotism.

This is the end of the American Dream: when the world is out of control, you make believe that it is not. You look out with blinded eyes and smile, and Milo Minderbinder embraces you. "Matters of behavior," worse than being meaningless, are suicidal if there is nothing behind them. As Diver says, ostensibly speaking only of his own decline but really summing up what happened to the beliefs of the "old order" in the twentieth century, "The manner remains intact for some time after the morale cracks."

Tender Is the Night is about the cracking of the manner. The opposite of the brilliant sunshine of the beach is the darkness of the human soul. Not a Christian soul filled with visions of the Wordsworthian Paradise it left behind, but the soul of man filled with its dark, dangerous, yet beautiful dreams. It is the soul of the crook, which wants what it wants because it is, not because of what it wants to be. It is the soul of Tommy Barban, and of Williams's Jacataqua.

One should look at it with "crook's eyes," but "crook's eyes" or not, Fitzgerald is saying that man must look at it if he is going to live rather than just survive. Diver is forced by his profession to look into and try to solve the problems presented by the dark. He is a minister's son. He sees what his own dark nature is and feels guilty. He has been told that he is a Puritan, not a crook, and the discovery that his own manner is not merely at odds with but totally antithetical to his substance is too much for him. It turns him into a "mad Puritan." Better this than nothing.

Diver's goodbye to his fathers is a goodbye to a family, a heritage, a religion, and it is a goodbye to himself. Dick Diver learns who and what he is, and what he learns has absolutely nothing to do with other people. He is "on his own" in a much different sense from Jake Barnes, for what Diver has discovered about himself renders a pose impossible.

> "You're all so dull," he said.
> "But we're all there is!" cried Mary. "If you don't like nice people, try the ones who aren't nice, and see how you like that! All people want is to have a good time and if you make them unhappy you cut yourself off from nourishment."

This comes after Mary and Lady Caroline Sibly-Biers have dressed themselves as sailors and picked up young girls on the waterfront. There was a time when Dick considered himself a "nice person"—"lucky Dick," as he called himself in college. Of course, Mary is right; she and Caroline are nice, as nice as anybody can be.

Niceness, as important as it was to Diver's father, stands as a symbol to Dick of all that he must keep away from because he sees too clearly the rot beneath it. Drunk. The blessing he delivers over the beach carries with it the heartfelt wish that the fools under the umbrellas may continue to believe in themselves as "nice people." He makes the sign of the cross over them, absolving them of sins they know nothing of. Let Mary, perverse as she is, continue blind and bless her for it, but the Marys and Carolines are not for Diver. If he cannot be Barban or Nicole, he at least knows who he is.

Tommy Barban must act. When he feels that Nicole is insulted, he demands a duel; when the time is right, he takes Nicole; and when she wants to go to Dick, he is able to say ("pulling her down firmly"), "Let well enough alone." This is something that Dick Diver could never say. Fitzgerald wants us to admire Barban, as he wants us to admire Nicole for the miraculous discovery of strength she achieves. They are the "lucky" ones and it would be nice if everyone could do what they do ("Wouldn't it be pretty to think so?"), but everyone can't. Along with the actors, there are those possessed of a mind, with the need to think if they are to live. Diver is one of these. What is wrong with people like Mary Minghetti is that they want pity. They think, but they think wrong. They think that the world is watching and judging them, and they don't understand that the world is totally unconcerned with them. Both the Barbans and the Divers understand this. The difference between them is that Tommy acts, and Dick tries to know.

Tommy acts because he possesses by nature those "dark truths" that Diver discovers so painfully. To him, desire is not evil; it is merely natural. The whole healing process that Nicole Diver undergoes is really the process of learning to understand herself and make herself ready for Barban. What Nicole learns is that if she actually wants another person, she must accept herself as she is without fear and guilt; that she cannot, as she did with Dick, turn to another for help. In her own way, she learns the isolation of the individual as well as does Diver. Nicole chooses survival, knowing full well what she is doing. Diver chooses to disappear, with equal knowledge.

Both Dick and Nicole are saved in the only real way man can be saved: by knowing who they are. Nicole knows that she had spent her life lying to herself, pretending that she felt guilt, pretending that she was a Puritan, and Dick knows that he, too, had spent his life pretending that he wasn't a Puritan, that he was a scientist, beyond and impervious to guilt. So man is an isolated animal, estranged, with no hope for either Heaven or Hell. And, really, if history has lied to him, it is his own fault for believing it.

Tender Is the Night is the refutation, nineteen centuries after Paul of Tarsus, of the hopes and illusions offered by Christianity. America in the nineteenth century was the Christian nation in the course of history. Nowhere else in either time or space had the teaching of Paul been put into such perfect social and economic harmony; never had the basic Pauline-Puritan attitude toward the world ("Succeed. And if you don't, don't cry; it's your own fault. Smile. Be nice. Heaven is still there") been accepted and executed by so many people, and never so successfully. But what Barban knows by instinct and the Divers learn is that that attitude is, quite simply, false, and that it has nothing to do with life.

The falseness of the façade of the Puritan ethic is exposed in incident after incident and relationship after relationship in *Tender Is the Night*. Successful, diligent Mr. Warren ("a fine American type in every way") goes to bed with his youngest daughter; at Abe North's drunken departure from Paris, the crowd of Americans at the station, with their "frank new faces, intelligent, considerate, thoughtless, fought-for," is suddenly shocked when one of its members, Maria Wallis, pulls a revolver from her purse and shoots an Englishman, while Abe waves obliviously from the moving train; Abe North is beaten to death in a New York speakeasy, just able to crawl home to the Racquet Club to die; and Mary North, still considering herself "nice people," is arrested for picking up young girls. The manner is cracked, and the dark side of man, hidden as sin for so many centuries, peeks out anywhere and at any time. If Dick, upon hearing of Abe's death, weeps for the past, he does not cry sentimental tears. He is not bemoaning the loss of innocence; rather he is cursing the fact that he ever had the illusion of it.

Rosemary Hoyt is naïve; she is not innocent. She thinks of Dick as a substitute father and she wants to go to bed with him. As much as she adores the whole Diver way of life, she knows precisely what it is. When she triumphantly announces that she has arranged a screen test for Dick, with the hopes that she will be able to co-star in a movie with him, the others are shocked at her naïve lack of discretion. Naïve, yes. Indiscreet, yes. But totally correct. What Rosemary finds so wonderful about the world of the Divers is that it is exactly like a movie: pretty, sparkling, gay, with a happy ending guaranteed. Being with them is like watching *Daddy's Girl.* There is the same relationship between the life the Divers seem to live and their real lives as there is between the lives of the characters on the screen in *Daddy's Girl* and the lives of the actors playing them when off the screen. The reason that Rosemary's announcement shocks is that she is saying "Since your life is an act, why not get paid for it?"

The carefree beauty of the Divers is a marvelously crafted illusion. The joy that Rosemary sees in it is, like the feeling of joy that a moviegoer experiences, in her and not in them. The feeling of comfort and safety that a good Christian man is supposed to feel in the bosom of his family and with his friends is here no more than fake. What saves the Divers is that they are aware they are wearing masks. What damns Mary North Minghetti is that she believes hers is real.

The "American way of life" in *Tender Is the Night* is the basis for a movie scenario, and the American Dream is precisely that. The night is real and it cannot be avoided. In fact, if man is to live, it must be sought, and understood if not embraced. It *is* better to be a "sane crook," but if we cannot be that, at the very least we must face the fact that we are "mad Puritans." We are asked to assume the incredible burden of finding out who we are no matter what the cost. The road to knowledge moves inward, and we are asked to travel it with honest, open eyes. Anything else would be suicide. And *Tender Is the Night* is about real life and real death. Poses no longer work, solutions do not console. And madness comes back with Ahab still lashed to the whale's side, grimacing.

ELIOT
ROSEWATER

Eliot Rosewater sits in squalor, getting fat and drinking Southern Comfort, because his grandfathers realized that acting like that was no way to get ahead, and that people who acted that way could be "taken." He buys fire engines because, in the process of becoming a decorated hero in the Second World War, he led a raid on a burning clarinet factory in Bavaria and personally killed three unarmed peasant firemen, including a boy who "didn't look more than fourteen." He gives the end of the Foundation money to all the bastard children of Rosewater County, claiming them as his own, "regardless of blood type," because to him they really are.

It's only sad that Eliot Rosewater had to become God in order to do something good.

"And Eliot became a drunkard, a Utopian dreamer, a tinhorn saint, an aimless fool." In his secret, locked-up letter to the imaginary relatives who will inherit the Foundation upon his death, this is the way that Eliot sums himself up, looking upon himself through the eyes of the world. He is right. He is also right, as are all fools, dreamers, saints, and drunkards, when he says, "Be a sincere, attentive friend of the poor." But in a society based upon the idea that the poor deserve to be that way, because they didn't want to succeed enough to make it, it is not easy to be a good Samaritan. Go too far and you get locked up as insane. When a young lawyer named Norman Mushari finds out about the Rosewater Foundation and how much money it has, he knows immediately that Eliot is insane (insanity being the only way a Rosewater can be relieved as head of the Foundation): after all, foundation funds are for physicists not barbers, political scientists not firemen; any man who gives money away without receiving fame for his sacrifice has to be crazy. Norman Mushari searches through the Rosewater family files looking for a Rosewater desperate enough for money to want to commit a relative to an asylum and foolish enough to give Norman an attractive cut. He finds him in the person of pathetic, sleazy, Fred Rosewater, busy whoring his life away selling insurance to laborers in Rhode Island.

Fred stirred his coffee. "I wouldn't be anything without my bride, and I know it." His bride was named Caroline. Caroline was the mother of an unattractive, fat little boy, poor little Franklin Rosewater. Caroline had taken lately to drinking lunch with a rich Lesbian named Amanita Buntline.

"I've done what I can for her," Fred declared. "God knows it isn't enough. Nothing could be enough." There was a real lump in his throat. He knew that lump had to be there and it had to be real, or he wouldn't sell any insurance. "It's something, though, something even a poor man can do for his bride."

Fred rolled his eyes mooningly. He was worth forty-two thousand dollars dead.

One of the major problems faced by our forefathers was the relationship between life and death. What, precisely, were we working for in this life? Should our eyes be directed toward Heaven or earth? How much would "the works of this world" amount to when it came time for the "Divine Accounting"? Insurance solved most, if not all, of the problem. Heaven or Hell for us, our brides and progeny could be taken care of for "only a few pennies a month." A basic theological problem could easily be solved by a half-way decent accountant with a computer; you put in so much, and when you died, so much went out. In the main, what's put in far exceeds what goes out, but then that's only good business. And good business is precisely what Fred Rosewater and Norman Mushari understand, and what Eliot Rosewater never has a chance of or a desire to understand. That's why Eliot is crazy and Fred and Mushari sane: basic economics.

Jonathan Edwards talked of man in the Eye of God as being as abhorrent and as tenuous in his existence as the spider is in the eye of man; Fred and Norman feel exactly the same way, save that, instead of damning and putting the fear of Hell into the spider, they'll insure him, and hope that when his web is finally cut, they'll take home a profit.

What makes Eliot Rosewater legally insane is the fact that he is interested in people's lives, not their deaths, in making them feel secure, not frightened. In a competitive society, that attitude is suicidal. Eliot doesn't care.

Yossarian witnessed death, learning Snowden's terrible secret; Lonelyhearts realized the ugliness of the despair of the crippled human heart; Quentin Compson felt the horror of his sister's "soiled pants"; on and on; but Eliot Rosewater looked into the face of an innocent whom he himself had slaughtered. He learns the awful lesson of the mortality of man by destroying man himself. And he learns the lessons of war, learns that they are the same as the lessons of peace. It makes no difference under what aegis you kill a man, he dies nonetheless.

> The Second World War was over—and there I was at high noon, crossing Times Square with a Purple Heart on.

He had a "Purple Heart on" all right, but the medal was accompanied by a nervous collapse from having bayoneted a fourteen-year-old boy in the throat.

Ours is not a religious society. A religious society respects the right of man, at least, to exist. Ours doesn't; instead, in a corruption of already corrupt Calvinism, it elects the eligibles; they go on, the others must be dealt with to the best of our abilities. And if they are dealt with harshly by one of the elect and if the dealing with has deleterious effects on the member of our side, then we can solve the matter by saying that our man has suffered a nervous collapse, or nerve damage, or a partial breakdown due to his war experiences. It's a very easy way out, and a Purple Heart is a very easy medal to get. But what about awarding a Purple Mind instead? That's what Eliot Rosewater should have received.

If a soldier's body is crippled in "the service of his country," he is richly, if temporarily, rewarded; but if his mind is crippled by the crime of taking another's life, he is condemned unless he makes an immediate and total recovery. Murder must never affect one's tennis game.

Sane means conformity to the norm, or, going back to the Founding Fathers once again, dedicating one's life to a pattern composed of a vague combination of self-aggrandizement and social continuity. Insane means living according to one's own moral code, without the proper sense of historicity. So it made no difference to the examining doctors that Eliot Rosewater didn't know what he was doing while he was in the hospital—he was doing what he was supposed to do, and that was enough to prove his sanity.

"I look at these people, these Americans," Eliot went on, "and I realize that they can't even care about themselves any more—because they have no *use*. The factory, the farms, the mines across the river—they're almost completely automatic now. And America doesn't even need these people for war—not any more. Sylvia—I'm going to be an artist."

"An artist?"

"I'm going to love these discarded Americans, even

67

though they're useless and unattractive. *That* is going to be my work of art."

One, maybe, could make a halfway decent case for the fears and war-like actions of the first settlers; they were, after all, scared foreigners. But since then our scared foreigners have been used for different purposes. Not really allowed to settle and develop, the late arrivals have been used for various purposes: labor, until they are automated out; war, when cannon fodder is needed; other than that, they are dumped in places like Rosewater, Indiana, where they can learn to hate each other in isolation. Eliot's great-grandfather Noah's life and times:

> When the United States of America, which was meant to be a Utopia for all, was less than a century old, Noah Rosewater and a few men like him demonstrated the folly of the Founding Fathers in one respect: those sadly recent ancestors had not made it the law of the Utopia that the wealth of each citizen should be limited. This oversight was engendered by a weak-kneed sympathy for those who loved expensive things, and by the feeling that the continent was so vast and valuable, and the population so thin and enterprising, that no thief, no matter how fast he stole, could more than mildly inconvenience anyone.
>
> Noah and a few like him perceived that the continent was in fact finite, and that venal office-holders, legislators in particular, could be persuaded to toss up great hunks of it for grabs, and to toss them in such a way as to have them land where Noah and his kind were standing.
>
> Thus did a handful of rapacious citizens come to control all that was worth controlling in America. Thus was the savage and stupid and entirely inappropriate

and unnecessary and humorless American class system created.

Honest, industrious, peaceful citizens were classed as bloodsuckers, if they asked to be paid a living wage. And they saw that praise was reserved henceforth for those who devised means of getting paid enormously for committing crimes against which no laws had been passed. Thus the American dream turned belly up, turned green, bobbed to the scummy surface of cupidity unlimited, filled with gas, went *bang* in the noonday sun.

E pluribus unum is surely an ironic motto to inscribe on the currency of this Utopia gone bust, for every grotesquely rich American represents property, privileges, and pleasures that have been denied the many. An even more instructive motto, in the light of history made by the Noah Rosewaters, might be: *Grab much too much, or you'll get nothing at all.*

Greed is natural to man. It used to be possible to treat it comically, to show the miser "getting his." It is no longer so. The idea of possessing for the sake of protection in this country has so far transcended the idea of mere greed as to make the term obsolete. In the eyes of most Americans, there is nothing either funny or wrong with wanting—indeed, needing—to have more than your neighbor. If some of us feel that competition to the point of killing is madness, there are many more of us who feel that certain deaths are necessary, so long as those deaths are not our own.

America has not invented a new language, but it has limited the connotations of certain words; success, for instance. Success means responding properly to a given set of circumstances, or, more precisely, making a lot of money and then holding on to it. The sane are successful, the insane are not. The indigent don't even count. The only problem with them is that they won't all die. America wants desperately to be Sparta, but unfortunately we've given so much pap to the rest of the world about a "working democracy" that we can't—or, at least, haven't yet been able to—develop a viable way to dispose of the "unfit" we either invited or forced to come to this country.

We have perfected the idea of condescension that we inherited from our British ancestors. So long as certain people representing certain groups realize their real position vis-à-vis what's going on, we'll give them money in exchange for their promise to tell the rest of their group that everything is basically all right. As long as they are ready to sell out what they should believe in for estates on the Hudson, the system will survive. And nobody, of any race, creed, or color, has, as yet, really "blown the whistle."

Protection of the system is the real function of foundations, and that is precisely what Eliot Rosewater cannot understand. Eliot feels guilty, and sets about in his own small way to try to repay the debts, in loss of human dignity and death, incurred by both his ancestors and himself. Eliot wants not to compete. He realizes that what he has comes from the very finite world of hurt and frustrated humanity. And so he tries to give back to his world what it should have had to begin with. What he doesn't realize is that money is not what man should have. Although people can be bought off, and be offered a Daddy in the form of a drunk who can be reached by telephone at any hour of the day or night, money and a voice that professes to understand have nothing to do with human dignity, which is precisely what the disenfranchised lack, and no amount of condescension, no matter how well meant, can give it to them.

Eliot, sane in his desires, is as insane as Miss Lonely-hearts in his method of executing them. Making a "work of art" out of loving the poor and discarded is as selfishly crazy as telling them that it is their own fault that they are unwanted and that they should suffer more in order to truly appreciate the state of their desperation.

The rich may be able to be friends of the poor, giving them some of the money that time and greed took from them, but being friends with them is out of the question in America, because America is a "land of opportunity" and one cannot be friends with another if he either covets what the other has or feels sorry for the other's failure; the lion simply cannot lie down with the lamb, to say nothing of the lion envisioning himself as the shepherd. Uncas must die again so that Natty Bumppo can die once, peacefully, only age finally stopping him; rocking gracefully into eternity.

Eliot and Lonelyhearts talk about *them*, whether "they" be the hurt and the ugly of Lonelyhearts's world, or the poor of Eliot Rosewater's. An inferior they which a superior me feels honor-bound to try to help. So we end up with one me as a demented Christ demanding suffering, and another me as God the Father, madly giving the only thing he has, his money, to his children. And the trees of the new Garden of Eden have leaves of green paper.

As Reed McAllister, a senior partner in McAllister, Robjent, Reed & McGee, told Stewart Buntline—husband of Amanita, the lesbian—some twenty years before Eliot's final breakdown, when Stewart, a starry-eyed and confused sophomore-to-be at Harvard, came to him with the idea that he wanted to give his fourteen-million-dollar fortune to the poor:

"History tells us this, my dear young Mr. Buntline, if it tells us nothing else: Giving away a fortune is a futile and destructive thing. It makes whiners of the poor, without making them rich or even comfortable. And the donor and his descendants become undistinguished members of the whining poor. . . .

"Cling to your miracle, Mr. Buntline. Money is dehydrated Utopia. This is a dog's life for almost everybody, as your professors have taken such pains to point out. But, because of your miracle, life for you and yours can be a paradise! Let me see you smile! Let me see that you already understand what they do not teach at Harvard until the junior year: That to be born rich and to stay rich is something less than a felony."

The history lesson took with Stewart Buntline: not quite forty, he sleeps and drinks in his study, an unopened fifty-seven-dollar railroad atlas of the Civil War on his lap, looking like a drunken cross between "Cary Grant and a German shepherd," with only his little daughter checking periodically to see if he is still alive. While at the same time, Eliot Rosewater, whose only real experience with history was the murder of some Bavarian firemen, sits half a continent away giving his money away by phone to anyone who asks for it. Old McAllister was right. It doesn't make very much sense to give away your fortune, particularly if it's the only one you have.

But why, for God's sake, is it necessary to have a fortune in the first place? Is rapacity, pure greed, the only verification of sanity?

Yes.

We can call Vonnegut anything we wish, label him a satirist, black humorist, fantasist, just so long as we are

72

aware that he is first of all a realist—he is talking about the morality of the world as it is, and of this country as we have developed and perfected it. If it is a world of rich, hollowed-out Stewart Buntlines and sadly, inefficiently mad Eliot Rosewaters on one side and snarling, hate-filled, mistrustful poor masses on the other, with mini-men like Norman Mushari conniving and manipulating in the middle—well, it is still ours. Our forefathers began it all for us by discovering their unlimited greed before they discovered the Mississippi River. Not even the sacrifice of a fortune as large as Eliot Rosewater's can do anything about that. Because *that* is the real American Dream. Rerun the film again. It still ends the same way. You can't stop Ahab's screaming or tell Arthur Dimmesdale that it's all right, and Dick Diver has disappeared in the small towns that the fortunes of American rich men have brought forth in upper New York State.

When Humbert Humbert crossed and recrossed the American continent with and without his Lo, he saw what Americans had done to the land they "found" and made their own: the myriad of conveniences they had contrived to make the process of getting through a life easier. Since his journeys, things have gotten even better: cars are faster, roads are straighter, there is color TV, air conditioning is everywhere, and beautiful golden airplanes fill our skies. But one still needs money to enjoy the largesse of his fellows. This is what Eliot Rosewater recognized, and what he tried to offer in one small corner of this country. He bought people TV sets, and the things they saw advertised on them. He tried to create a small Utopia within the fabric of mid-twentieth-century America, where the poor could have all the crap that the middle class possessed without the worry of payments. But the crap remained just that: useless hair processes, electric can openers, plastic war toys for the kids—even, for Nazi sympathizer Lincoln Ewald, "a cheap phonograph and a set of German lessons on records." Utopias are not built around an increasing number of possessions; or, at least, one would hope that the Sears, Roebuck catalogue or the television commercial would not dictate the standards of the ideal society. But Eliot chose to build his garden according to what its tenants wanted, and what they wanted was what others had, or what they thought others wanted. The whole point of Eliot Rosewater's failure is the grotesque proportion of the greed promulgated by the system in which he tried to work: he only wanted to give the deprived what others with more money had, and they grabbed the bait with all the ardor of the dumbest fish.

But God dies periodically, so it isn't a good idea to be too dependent upon Him, and an even worse idea to try to be Him. This is the lesson Diana Moon Glampers learns when she catches Eliot just as he is about to board the bus leaving Rosewater, Indiana, for the last time. She carries her white Princess telephone, a gift from the Rosewater Foundation, and smashes it on the pavement beside the bus. She smashes it because once Eliot is gone there is nobody for her to call any more, and certainly nobody to call her. When Eliot tells her, "You could join some church group, perhaps," she can only cry:

> "*You're* my church group! You're my *everything!* You're my government. You're my husband. You're my friends."

It is very difficult to form a religious order if you're not prepared to, particularly if, as is the case with Eliot, "these claims" make you "uncomfortable" and your last word can only be:

> "You're very nice to say so. Good luck to you. I really have to be going now." He waved "Good-bye."

Eliot's wife, Sylvia, leaves because he was "too good," after she suffered a nervous collapse and burned the Rosewater firehouse down. Her psychiatrist, a young man named Dr. Ed Brown, made his reputation on the diagnosis of her collapse, which he described as "Samaritrophia," or, in lay terms, "The hell with you, Jack, I've got mine!"

Dr. Brown refers to Eliot and Sylvia as "Mr. and Mrs. Z. of Hometown, U.S.A.," and describes Eliot:

> "As for Mr. Z: He is certainly sick too, since he certainly isn't like any other man I never knew. He will not leave Hometown, except for very short trips as far as Indianapolis and no farther. I suspect that he cannot leave Hometown. Why not?
>
> To be utterly unscientific and science becomes nauseating to a therapist after a case such as this: His Destination is there."

His Destination wasn't there, because Eliot and the world, between them, wouldn't let it be there. No sane society can allow a man to take a vast fortune and bestow it on the indigents, and no sane man would ever try to do it as overtly as did Eliot Rosewater; if you want to give your money away, you give it to people who don't need it, and then make a lot of noise about the amount of the sum; you never let it dribble out for record players, or even fire engines, and then never say anything until somebody questions you about it. Maybe, in some other time and some other place, if there really were such a place as "Hometown, U.S.A.," "Mr. Z." could have his destination there, but he would have to really belong there.

It is very doubtful that any of us will ever see "Hometown" or be "Mr. Z."

LONELYHEARTS

Although his cheap clothes had too much style, he still looked like the son of a Baptist minister. A beard would become him, would accent his Old-Testament look. But even without a beard no one could fail to recognize the New England puritan. His forehead was high and narrow. His nose was long and fleshless. His bony chin was shaped and cleft like a hoof. On seeing him for the first time, Shrike had smiled and said, "The Susan Chesters, the Beatrice Fairfaxes and the Miss Lonelyhearts are the priests of twentieth-century America."

Diver was full, red, and open in his American looks. Lonelyhearts is sparse and gaunt. While Diver suggests Cape Cod summers, Lonelyhearts means harsh Vermont winters. If, in the angularity of his face, he suggests the stern self-righteousness of his father, there is also in him the warped thirst for love of his mother. Shrike is frighteningly correct when he lumps Lonelyhearts, Susan Chester, and Beatrice Fairfax together as "the priests of twentieth-century America." The Puritan conscience got confused and mixed mother-love and discipline, and Lonelyhearts wants to love the people who write him letters, but can't because they are naughty children. A real priest is trained not to love in the personal sense, but to feign a love from a distance for his "flock." A mother loves by instinct, and in a very personal sense. When you mix the roles, you end up with a creature compelled, driven by a desire to love everyone in a personal sense, yet inadequate, if not repelled, whenever anyone gets too close.

What Lonelyhearts wants to achieve in his "Imitation of Christ" is a sacrifice of himself for the principle of love, by which he means he wants to die because he hates other people, that the touch of another human being is repugnant to him. His messianic impulse is not the urge for self-sacrifice for the mankind he loves better than they will ever know; it is the urge for self-destruction of the mother who feels herself unnatural because she can't bring herself to love her deformed child.

Lonelyhearts is mad. He looks at himself and finds himself inadequate. Not guilty but inadequate. He cannot do what he wants to do and feels that there must be a way to overcome his problem. The more Shrike mocks him, the more Lonelyhearts turns to his notion of Christ. He even recrucifies his own Christ, taking it off its small wooden cross and nailing it with spikes to his wall, but "Instead of writhing, the Christ remained calmly decorative."

> He knew now what this thing was—hysteria, a snake whose scales are tiny mirrors in which the dead world takes on a semblance of life. And how dead the world is . . . a world of doorknobs. He wondered if hysteria were really too steep a price to pay for bringing it to life.

"This thing" is Lonelyhearts's Christ fixation. He knows that Shrike's reasoned badgering has rendered any sane approach to Christ impossible, and at this early point in his deterioration, he still has the ability to wonder if madness is too great a price to pay for Christianity. Lonelyhearts is a truly "mad Puritan." His insanity comes from the desperate urge to be good, not from the recognition that being good is impossible of a Dick Diver. His lust for Christ is precisely that. He can experience Him only in an evocation of dark pre-Christian mysteries. He chants "Christ, Christ, Jesus Christ. Christ, Christ, Jesus Christ," relishing the words, believing that his ivory Christ has the ability to bleed. It is the blood of "the mystery" that Lonelyhearts wants and it is the blood that terrifies him. He remembers a drunken attempt at the sacrifice of a lamb that happened in college. Despite his incantation of Christ's name, the rite turned out a disaster. The knife broke and the lamb crawled off into the bushes, where Lonelyhearts later crushed its head with a stone. There was blood, but it was untransformed. No mystery, just a slow, ugly dying.

With his cynical, rational eyes, this is what Shrike sees in life. He is not satanic. He simply knows that there is no help for the world. When man faces man, most knives break, and, if there are no bushes to wait in, it is still the stone that crushes us. Things die, not beautifully, but gradually gagging on their own blood. The process of living is the process of dying and nothing brings a mysterious beauty into it. The fact that Shrike is mean, ugly, and totally self-interested has nothing to do with the fact that he is able to survive. That he does is West's comment on the nature of the world in which we live. A world where the Lonelyhearts are driven mad and the Shrikes prosper. A world where the word "love" is no more meaningful or joyful than the consumptive's final cough.

America's Puritanism made it possible for the country to become the most powerful nation in the world. But as its power increased, its individuals disappeared. In our frontier society, one built forts because of the fear of enemies waiting beyond the next hill. The people banded together for safety and convinced themselves that they were necessary one to the other. It makes no difference whether this society was the church of the seventeenth century, where the enemy was man's increasing knowledge of the universe, or the American West of the nineteenth century, where the enemy was the very visible Indian; the problem is the same: there is something dangerous out there and we can only protect ourselves against it by standing strong and shoulder to shoulder. But as the power of either church or nation increases, defense against the enemy must decrease, because once the enemy is either dead or harmlessly absorbed, the weapons of defense have an ugly propensity of turning inward, wreaking more havoc on the hands that hold them than any external enemy could ever have done.

Unfortunately the attitude of the frontier brings to the minds of the power-hungry the irresistible illusion of permanence, the feeling that "I" can run the world. And so it is. From the simple and obvious stance of frightened people, we develop a principle of power and control, where the leaders, instead of trying to assuage fear, promulgate it, withholding knowledge in order to maintain control.

The key is training. The people must be given enough of either bread or facts to sustain them, but not enough to corrupt them. They must be trained to believe certain things about the reality and the possibility of their world and then held in certain specific postures, frozen, believing that they are moving forward. But the only movement is time, the rest static.

In his father's church, Lonelyhearts encountered Christianity. But it had no effect of control. On the contrary, he faced the blood and the dying of the Crucifixion with the wild passion of the first martyrs. He genuinely wanted Christ's death to be meaningful; he wanted to see the fact of death transformed into something spiritual and not remain the blunt end of existence. He wanted meaning. Lonelyhearts plunged into the faith of his fathers trying to find the substance he was so desperately sure must be there.

Shrike speaks for West: Lonelyhearts is a pathetic fool, sick in his head because he can't accept the world for the piece of shit that it is and himself as an effeminate, sickly adolescent.

Shrike is the real world, but that doesn't mean it's good. West is after the world that Shrike represents, a world where cynical acceptance is the only sane approach, a world where a love-haunted man like Lonelyhearts is driven to an insane suicide because he cannot accept his inability to love, a world which has systematically driven the humanity out of man. It is this vision of the world that marks the difference between a Fitzgerald and a West. Fitzgerald saw the world as bearable to the sane—in fact, good, if one could approach it properly. His Barbans function beautifully, and his Divers at least survive, richer for their knowledge. To West the world is unendurable: being sane means being Shrike; being sensitive means being Lonelyhearts. These are the only two approaches to the world left for the intelligent being; the others are all variations on the Doyles, stupid and groping. If Diver sounds like Dostoevski's Grand Inquisitor in declining to tell Mary North that she is not "nice people," Lonelyhearts wants so much to be Aloysha that it kills him.

With Jake Barnes we encounter cynicism, but it is a malleable type of cynicism. Barnes is, after all, basically a nice guy. If he knows the world is hopeless, he at least has the manners and consideration to keep his knowledge to himself. Shrike won't keep his mouth shut. He has a messianic mission: "This is the truth, foul as it is, accept it!" And there is ministerial glee in him. Lonelyhearts goes through "dark night of the soul" after "dark night of the soul" trying to escape the truth and grasp for what he wants to be true. Shrike seems all sunshine and poisonous flowers when he preaches his gospel. Barnes knows truths and wants to keep them to himself, work for peace, be a "steer among bulls." Shrike knows and wants everyone to accept the knowledge whether they can understand it or not. Shrike is not a black priest; there is no perversion in him. He merely speaks of the world as he sees and believes it. He does not try to cover up or delude his parishioners. He preaches, with a beautifully pristine, deliberate Calvinistic ruthlessness. It is not his fault if he drives his flock mad.

The central conflict of *Miss Lonelyhearts* is in the battle between Shrike's knowledge and Lonelyhearts's hope, and Shrike's knowledge coupled with Lonelyhearts's intelligence has, as Lonelyhearts knows only too well, "made a sane view of this Christ business impossible." Lonelyhearts comes to this conclusion after reading the words of Father Zossima in *The Brothers Karamazov,* praising love for all living creatures, a pure, all-embracing love which would free the lover for the purest of happiness. Yet what Lonelyhearts thinks about Zossima's idea of love is that it would make him "a big success. His column would be syndicated and the whole world would learn to love." And through his success the Kingdom of Heaven would arrive as the commercial and the religious mixed together, one dependent on the other, the fulfillment of the Puritan American Dream. All Shrike asks is that the religious hypocrisy be tossed out, that Lonelyhearts not try to say that there is any justification for his dream in the sense of bringing good to mankind. Shrike knows full well that the only reason for doing anything is self-aggrandizement, that the hope that he will be a success with a syndicated column is the believable part of Lonelyhearts's dream, but that it will never come to pass so long as he believes that the whole world could actually learn to love. He wants Lonelyhearts to believe in the possibility of the evolution of ideas as well as species, that it is possible to take the proven economic values of Puritanism and use them without feeling guilty for not enriching the spiritual life of the people one must use. Make money and forget that altruistic nonsense; realize that suckers are suckers, and that if you don't use them someone else will.

Lonelyhearts would be good. He would also be successful. "Put your hand on the radio." "Pay me." "Listen." But don't "take a healing." Suffer, sons of bitches, because you're worse than you ever dreamed you were. Jonathan Edwards with mass media in his bitter, shaking fists.

Shrike is "right reason" and he has no hope. He does not offer a way out, unless scorn is a solution. He simply describes the futility of hope, of any answer. Anywhere else, it is as bad as, if not worse than, it is here, and there is no way of changing anything. In fact, if one questions his motives carefully enough one will discover that he really doesn't want to change anything; he just thinks that it might be good if he did. This is what Lonelyhearts recognizes in Shrike's words. He realizes that his yearning for Christian altruism is a fraud; that his own vocation is really of a much different sort. He recognizes that his concern with his Christ is a fascination with the very real physical fact of bleeding and death; that he likes not so much the idea of transcendence as the preceding gore of the dying; that he would rather hurt than heal.

Lonelyhearts is a man who loves the suffering of others. Shrike is not the Antichrist of *Miss Lonelyhearts*; Lonelyhearts himself is. His Christianity is voyeurism. He wants his little ivory Christ to writhe and bleed on the wall. It won't, so he imagines it does. Shrike would offer cynical, offhanded pap to Lonelyhearts's pathetic, beseeching letter writers; he would tell them anything tongue-in-cheek to stop them from writing, but, in a strange paradox, the things that he suggests would also help them in their suffering, because he would treat them as the helpless fools that they are. And, desperate to believe anything, they would bless him with their haltness, lameness, and blindness. "Don't worry, you're not as ugly as you know you are." What Lonelyhearts would do is ask them to add a spiritual dimension to their physical suffering: instead of merely moaning, he wants them to really face the agony of emptiness, and die. So that he can watch.

In a sane, beneficent world, Lonelyhearts would be able to recognize and understand his nature. Lonelyhearts looks out at his world of cripples and criminals and feels that since he was raised to be a good Christian, he should do something for them. He should open their eyes to the reality of their suffering. This is the core of his madness. He thinks he wants to immerse himself in the groaning world around him, but the slightest touch of that world sends him into paroxysms of disgust.

Lonelyhearts is a hater corrupted. He should have been allowed the privilege of living his disgust privately. But he wanted to "make it," to accept the world and be accepted by it. He wanted to go to bed with Shrike's wife; he wanted to enjoy going to bed with Betty; he wanted to be able to stomach going to bed with Mrs. Doyle. "Wanted": that one, simple, plaintive word echoes throughout *Miss Lonelyhearts:* If only *I could.*

If Shrike appears to be evil, it is because he says "YOU CAN'T" with such reasoned authority. He is a hysterical hypocrite, but the world is run by hysterical hypocrites. They are the ones who survive and triumph. This is what

Shrike tries to tell Lonelyhearts, when, in much more than a "Temptation of Christ," he tries to explain to him and demonstrate by example exactly how the world works:

> "You spiritual lovers think that you alone suffer. But you are mistaken. Although my love is of the flesh flashy, I too suffer. It's suffering that drives me into the arms of the Miss Farkises of this world. Yes, I suffer."

Shrike knows who he is and, in a sense, revels in his lack of grace. Lonelyhearts knows only who he would be.

It is Lonelyhearts' final desperate immersion in Shrike's world, without Shrike's sight, that brings about his downfall.

Shrike, when talking to Doyle, asks him to tell them about humanity from his vantage point as a gas-meter inspector. Doyle, whom West describes as a "little cripple—a partially destroyed insect," responds with:

> "Everybody's got a frigidaire nowadays, and they say that we meter inspectors take the place of the iceman in the stories."

Shrike:

> "I can see, sir, that you are not the man for us. You know nothing about humanity: you are humanity. I leave you to Miss Lonelyhearts."

Shrike is right. It is only fitting and proper than an impotent "partially destroyed insect" should make a feeble, leering attempt at a joke about sexual prowess. Doyle is humanity—the crippled, in mind as well as body, humanity of the twentieth century; desperate, hopefully writing letters under the veil of anonymity and yet forced to break through that veil in a dim hope of some human contact. Destroyed, not ennobled by the world.

The American Dream come true, bringing with it madness and shame for the unfortunate, to whom the world is a bitterly critical mirror. Making them aware at all times of their ugliness and inadequacy. Even before television brought the miracle of perfectly formed bodies into every living room, where potbellied men, sweating in sleeveless undershirts, and their unattractive, gone-to-seed, pin-curled wives could watch, each disdaining the other, the lithe and the brilliant tell them that they, too, could be beautiful—even before this, the ugly of our always-expanding economy *knew* that they were ugly, and, even more appalling, they knew that it was their own fault, and here the madness of Lonelyhearts becomes the most abhorrently manifest. He tells the Doyles that if they love Christ—and, through Christ, each other—they will become beautiful. The Puritan minister has become an insane TV pitchman, Cotton Mather reincarnate in Bert Parks, and the Doyles know it. To Mrs. Doyle, Lonelyhearts's chatter about Christ and love means only that she wants to go to bed with him, and to Mr. Doyle that he has a friend who will play a little bit of faggy hanky-pank with him without daring to show his disgust. When Lonelyhearts screams his "Christ Is Love" message, Fay Doyle only says, "You were a scream with your fly open."

To the Doyles, and not only the Doyles of the crippled, poverty-stricken nineteen-thirties but the Doyles of any time and any place, "Christ Is Love" is nonsense. Christ is one thing, love is another, without a capital "L."

Lonelyhearts, in his last attempt to write his column:

Christ died for you.
He died nailed to a tree for you. His gift to you is

suffering and it is only through suffering that you can know Him. Cherish this gift, for . . .

This is his love. To Lonelyhearts, the Crucifixion is not only a justification for suffering, it is a demand for it. Christ becomes not the Saviour but "the black fruit that hangs on the crosstree," and Lonelyhearts, in his desperation to purify his Christ lust, joins hands with Satan in a beautifully executed Black Mass, urging man to accept the darkness of Christ so that he may suffer his way to a grisly death. "Suffer, damn you," he is saying, "because you don't deserve to live."

But the Doyles don't want to suffer; they don't want to die. They want to grab whatever tacky pleasures they can before life ends. They want to believe that they are "all right" so that they can pluck more forbidden fruits. Where Lonelyhearts fails most grievously as a priest is in the fact that he offers only negation, not salvation; he is talking about dying, not about being resurrected; he is talking about dead-end death for its own sake to people who only want life, who turn to him because they want answers for their pain, a way out, not a demand to bleed. They don't want a priest; they want a healer. So when Shrike tells Lonelyhearts to feed their illusions, offer them foolishness, like art, that they can believe in, he is much more right than wrong. The girl with no nose wants to be told where she can find one, not told to pray and to relish her suffering. And Doyle, when he comes up the stairs to Lonelyhearts's apartment with a gun wrapped in newspaper, wants to bluff and then be let off the hook, not driven by Lonelyhearts's madness into killing him.

DR. O'CONNOR

Djuna Barnes's *Nightwood* moves through time in images. At first it seems like a nightmare pure and simple, and it would be easy, if terrifying, to dismiss it as such. But *Nightwood* is much more than a very bad dream. It deals with the harsh light of reality, of the day, as much as it does with the fantasies of the night.

When Dick Diver tells Rosemary Hoyt that one-thirty in the afternoon is "not one of the worst times of the day," he is telling her that he has seen the worst times and that they do not, or should not, occur in the white, glaring sunlight of the beach. Diver is talking about the visible "worst times," the "worst times" of the manner, not the perpetual "dark night of the soul" of the pitifully, permanently cracked morale. He is talking of the darkness of nights with Nicole sobbing in the bathroom. Jake Barnes, too, hates the real, lonely night. He cries in his bed, alone, with the lights out. Lonelyhearts succumbs to the night, letting it feed his madness, clenching his fists and closing his eyes violently, making his plaster Christ bleed in his mind. Dr. O'Connor is the night.

Felix Volkbein's needs are simple. He only wants history to be real, something he can bow down to, a purposeful past, a plot through time. So he searches for glimpses of royalty, remnants of a heritage, solid, with names and positions holding through time. Born of a woman who died in childbirth at the age of forty-five, sired by a father who died of dandyism even before his birth, he had no history:

> His aunt, combing her long braids with an amber comb, told him what she knew, and this had been her only knowledge of his past. What had formed Felix from the date of his birth to his coming to thirty was unknown to the world.

Nora Flood only wants to pity:

> Nora had the face of all people who love the people —a face that would be evil when she found out that to love without criticism is to be betrayed. Nora robbed herself for everyone; incapable of giving herself warning, she was continually turning about to find herself diminished. Wandering people the world over found her profitable in that she could be sold for a price forever, for she carried her betrayal money in her own pocket.

"There was no ignominy in her; she recorded without reproach or accusation, being shorn of self-reproach or self-accusation." The condescension of the person who knows he's saved without thinking about it. She does not accuse others, because she cannot accuse herself. There is no greed in Nora, because there is no reflection in her. She is never really "taken" by anyone, because she offers herself first. She stands outside of life and time, uninvolved with movement, because each person and each event are of precisely the same importance to her. Until she meets Robin Vote.

Felix searched madly for a nonexistent heritage; Nora gave herself away without knowing. Jenny Petherbridge was an acquirer, "a squatter by instinct." Everything she owned, from tiny jade elephants to the passion of love, had at one time belonged to someone else. She was Nora's exact opposite, desperate to sweep the crumbs of existence off the world's tables and into her own pockets. Felix hoped to find the justification for his own existence and that of mankind somewhere in historical time. Nora stood blindly, at the summit. Jenny, rat-like, searched garbage cans to build a life for herself. They all loved Robin Vote.

> The perfume that her body exhaled was of the quality of that earth-flesh, fungi, which smells of captured dampness and yet is so dry, overcast with the odour of oil of amber, which is an inner malady of the sea, making her seem as if she had invaded a sleep incautious and entire. Her flesh was the texture of plant life, and beneath it one sensed a frame, broad, porous and sleep-worn, as if sleep were a decay fishing her beneath the visible surface. About her head there was an effulgence as of phosphorous glowing about the circumference of a body of water—as if her life lay through her in un-

gainly luminous deteriorations—the troubling structure of the born somnambule, who lives in two worlds—meet of child and desperado.

That state of both innocence and depravity ("meet of child and desperado") represents a point of existence that is before the Fall, a point where there is no distinction between good and evil, where the day and the night dance together, unafraid. Robin, "La Somnambule," goes through her life—"her dream" as O'Connor would call it—innocent because people relate to her, people need her, people use her, while she "can't do anything in relation to anyone but herself." Until the very end:

> Then she began to bark also, crawling after him— barking in a fit of laughter, obscene and touching. The dog began to cry then, running with her, head-on with her head, as if slowly and surely to circumvent her; soft and slow his feet went padding. He ran this way and that, low down in his throat crying, and she grinning and crying with him; crying in shorter and shorter spaces, moving head to head, until she gave up, lying out, her hands beside her, her face turned and weeping; and the dog too gave up then, and lay down, his eyes bloodshot, his head flat along her knees.

Man is asked to choose between the child and the desperado, between "obscene and touching." It is impossible for a human being to grin and cry at the same time. As Nicole Diver learns, there are sane crooks and mad Puritans, but the twain never meet. There are night people and day people, knaves and gulls; good is that, and evil that; and so on, and so on, and so on. Choose. Robin simply finally says "No," or, rather, she never says "Yes." She experiments with Felix, Nora, and Jenny, looking at their ways of living and finds them wrong or, at least, lacking. Barnes has placed Robin in a unique position. She has all the equipment of an adult human being and the experiences, but an unformed soul. The name Vote is no accident. She has yet to make her vow or cast her ballot for mankind. And, at the end, it is the dog she chooses.

The transvestite unlicensed gynecologist, Dr. Matthew O'Connor, knows all this from the very first, as he knows everything. He is the watchman of the night, the voice of the night, and, finally, the very night itself. It is he who officiates at Robin's almost birth as,

> with professional roughness, brought to a pitch by his eternal fear of meeting with the law (he was not a licensed practitioner), [he] said: "Slap her wrists, for Christ's sake. Where in hell is the water pitcher!"

Both birth and baptism, in both Heaven and Hell.

Dr. Matthew O'Connor delivered Nora Flood to her life in this world, and he forces Robin Vote to emerge from her pre-human trance:

> A series of almost invisible shudders wrinkled her skin as the water dripped from her lashes, over her mouth and on to the bed. A spasm of waking moved upward from some deep-shocked realm, and she opened her eyes. Instantly she tried to get to her feet. She said, "I was all right," and fell back into the pose of her annihilation.

Imagine the infant being baptized as not an infant at all, or as an infant who, although it had no idea of what it was, had knowledge of the world around it. A dark knowledge, dark enough to know that a trance was preferable to waking, that damnation was preferable to salvation, that the world of man was a place not to be. So that with this knowledge, the infant can say, "I was all right." "*Was.*" If one is truly able to choose, why choose original sin and all the resultant guilt? Why not remain in the trance? "Prove to me that my baptism means something. Show me that it is better to be human than to be a beast, if one has to be at all." Robin marries her Jew, but the Divine does not do for her what He did for Mary. He offers instead sick, miniature Guido, delivered in spite of the imprecations of the unwilling mother. She has her love affair with Christian charity, and ends it crushing a doll's head under her heel. And she immerses herself in the grubbing pathos of Jenny, only to be beaten savagely and bloodily in the back of a hansom. The world does not take care of those who are not its own. Use or be used. If Kierkegaard leapt one way, and Robin the other, who is to say who was right?

Dr. O'Connor.

O'Connor is "damned, and carefully public," to use his own words. To use more of them:

> "For Christ's sweet sake!" he said, and his voice was a whisper. "Now that you have all heard what you wanted to hear, can't you let me loose now, let me go? I've not only lived my life for nothing but I've told it for nothing—abominable among the filthy people—I know, it's all over, everything's over, and nobody knows it but me—drunk as a fiddler's bitch—lasted too long—" He tried to get to his feet, gave it up. "Now," he said, "the end—mark my words—now *nothing, but wrath and weeping!*"

God and Satan, priest and pervert, O'Connor is the world. A muddled, sick Tiresias, he is cursed with sight that lets him see the physical world as well as the souls of men; with a knowledge that men never listen to his words, yet filled with the terrible urge to say them, he tells the truth and then is forced to call it a lie. He is all things to all men and nothing to himself: the Holy Ghost as a lay analyst.

Nightwood is about Robin Vote and Dr. Matthew O'Connor. Hovering at all times over Robin's pure existence is the Doctor's terrible knowledge, and the Doctor, holding his hatred of Robin like a broken mace, is forced to move through the real world he loathes and knows, telling his "lies" to people who don't want to hear them. Shrike sat poor mad Lonelyhearts down for a good talking-to, laughing up his sleeve at the sick bastard, yet, in a strange way, really trying to help him. He felt that Lonelyhearts could be saved for the world if only he could forget the "Christ nonsense." O'Connor does not feel that about Robin Vote. She is dangerous, particularly to the damned.

Robin refuses to lose her purity. She destroys people because she will not be taken. In her being she offers unlimited possibility, a perfect doll lacking only the breath of humanity. But, to her, dog's breath smells better. The dog, at least, has not been chewing on desperation.

When the lioness in the circus weeps as she looks at Robin, she is weeping out of pure animal pity, creature-feeling for the poor animal who has to have human form. But when Nora weeps, she is crying for herself, because she cannot have Robin. It is an impure act, perhaps the only one Nora ever commits, but it is humanly selfish. She wants Robin for herself, and in the wanting she gives herself away as a human being and inadvertently offers up her prize doll to the junkman. If, after all, even Nora, the great giver, wants to take, why shouldn't Robin go to Jenny Petherbridge?

Years later, Vladimir Nabokov told the story of Dolores Haze, a doll with her head torn off, who said all right to the real world when her dream went bust. If all her beloved wanted to do was to make dirty pictures—well, then, it just wasn't possible to realize "true love." Robin doesn't want a perfect human relationship brought to life out of a ladies' magazine. Her dream is her life. It is the responsibility of others to make her human, make her want something or someone.

That is why O'Connor hates her. If Miss Lonelyhearts was confused by Father Zossima, Dr. O'Connor is the Second Coming the Grand Inquisitor feared in a different, madder, more complicated world. "Abominable among the filthy people," he "tells" his life for nothing, offering darkness and his own perversion as salvation. Christ and Tiresias in one twisted, perverted body.

The Puritan ethic burns like an angry, flickering candle in *Nightwood*, and it is O'Connor's job to blow it out:

> "God, take my hand and get me up out of this great argument—the more you go against your nature, the more you will know of it—hear me, Heaven! I've done and been everything that I didn't want to be or do— Lord, put the light out—so I stand here, beaten up and mauled and weeping, knowing I am not what I thought I was, a good man doing wrong, but the wrong man doing nothing much, and I wouldn't be telling you about it if I weren't talking to myself. I talk too much because I have been made so miserable by what you are keeping hushed. I'm an old worn-out lioness, a coward in my

corner; for the sake of my bravery I've never been one thing that I am, to find out what I am! Here lies the body of Heaven. The mocking bird howls through the pillars of Paradise, O Lord! Death in Heaven lies couched on a mackerel sky, on her breast a helmet and at her feet a foal with a silent marble mane. Nocturnal sleep is heavy on her eyes."

So much for "Father, forgive them, they know not what they do." The world is a "great argument"; its Messiah is "the wrong man doing nothing much" and its God a dead dream.

Marlowe, in Joseph Conrad's *Heart of Darkness*, said that we "live in the flicker," and that we must lie to the living about the nature of the darkness surrounding us if we are to stay alive. It is much the same thing that Shrike advised Lonelyhearts to do, or that Jake Barnes does, or that Dick Diver accomplishes in his blessing of the beach. It is the responsibility of the man who is enlightened to the night to keep its darkness from his fellows, to become a false prophet, simply to prevent suicides. But in order to do it, one has to keep outside of the night himself. Shrike uses cynicism; Barnes a tired stoicism; Diver isolation. They are false Messiahs; none of them is the New Christ of the Night. O'Connor is.

"Oh, the new moon! When will she come riding?"

"She" won't, and O'Connor, although crucified, is never to be resurrected. The gate may very well be strait, but all O'Connor knows is that "God's chosen walk close to the wall," while he himself staggers wildly, publicly through the night. In an ideal time and place, O'Connor could just call his flock at sunset and be the Shepherd caring for his sheep, but the world of *Nightwood* is not ideal; it is real. So one of his sheep, Nora, can say to him: "You know what none of us know until we have died. You were dead in the beginning." And O'Connor replies:

> "And I was doing well enough, until you kicked my stone over, and out I came, all moss and eyes; and here I sit, as naked as only those things can be, whose houses have been torn away from them to make a holiday, and it my only skin—labouring to comfort you. Am I supposed to render up my paradise—that splendid acclimation—for the comfort of weeping women and howling boys?"

No frankincense and myrrh, just an unwilling Jesus, who cries:

> "Do you think, for Christ's sweet sake, that I am so happy that you should cry down my neck? Do you think there is no lament in this world, but your own? Is there not a forbearing saint somewhere? Is there no bread that does not come proffered with bitter butter? I, as good a Catholic as they make, have embraced every confection of hope, and yet I know well, for all our outcry and struggle, we shall be for the next generation not the massive dung fallen from the dinosaur, but the little speck left of a humming-bird. . . . Oh, you poor blind cow! Keep out of my feathers; you ruffle me the wrong way and flit about, stirring my misery! What end is sweet? Are the ends of the hair sweet when you come to number them?"

O'Connor feels that man is no more than a lizard given guilt and that, in trying to run from his guilt, he falls only into self-pity, wailing at the stars against pain. Guilt, self-pity, and pain: the human condition: the night. It is this that everyone asks O'Connor to save them from, but how can he, when Robin Vote refuses to fall? Every Eve must taste of the forbidden fruit and join with her Adam in the human dance. But Robin will not leave the Garden.

O'Connor is not Evil and Robin Good, or vice versa. They are not meant to represent qualities. They are what they are. O'Connor is the entire history and soul of mankind in one body. ("The reason I'm so remarkable is that I remember everyone even when they are not about.") His is an awesome responsibility: to know and be all sin and to know that his death would not bring even the possibility of absolution. He rants against the world that he is, knowing full well that his ranting can only be seen as the cheapest form of exhibitionism:

> "Funny little man," someone said. "Never stops talking—always getting everyone into trouble by excusing them because he can't excuse himself—the Squatting Beast, coming out at night."

"Damned," all right, and very "carefully public." Yet what a perfect description of the Saviour, "always getting everyone into trouble by excusing them because he can't excuse himself." Christ knew whose Son He was, and He set about to do "His Father's business." O'Connor isn't quite so sure of himself. He feels compelled, but it's to a messianic mission that he doesn't like, with an ending that terrifies him. "Wrath and weeping" is a far cry from the promise of the Kingdom, but then the New Jerusalem has turned out to be a whorehouse, and the only denizens of the Garden are animals.

It is no wonder that O'Connor hates Robin Vote. She is

everything that he can't be, while he is everything that she won't be. She declines the Knowledge of This World because it is repellent to her, and in so doing she denounces him—but not thrice; for the New Messiah, once is enough.

When O'Connor talks about Robin's "dream," he is talking about his own reality. He has drained every glass, save the one meant for Elijah, and a damned beast got to it before he could. From talking of the night, from saving people for it, he plunges into it. He has nowhere else to go. O'Connor knows the night for the real world that it is, and knows full well that accepting it offers the only salvation available to man. It is his job to convince the world of the full horror of its birthright, and then to prevent it from committing suicide.

O'Connor, as Christ, simply quits, hands in his letter of resignation to his world and says it's all over. There is no way to follow him, because there is no place for him to go. And there is no way to follow Robin Vote, for hers is the way of the beast, "grinning and crying simultaneously." Human beings can't do that, particularly Christian ones. O'Connor, as Christ, teaches us that simple fact. "Wrath and weeping": judgment and guilt: death and damnation. Accept it, mankind, it's the truth.

Djuna Barnes has early, dark roots, all the way back to poor Job, sitting on his heap while his angry, nasty God calls him worm. Man, in *Nightwood*, is worm, and his heap is more than he deserves. Yet he keeps asking questions and demanding answers. Nora demands that O'Connor tell her of the night, even though he says, "Beware of that dark door." O'Connor cannot shout her down. His voice lacks the resonance, if not the knowledge, of Yahweh's. He can only tell and retell his story to a world that wants something else and sing the dark songs of Jonathan Edwards slightly off-key. But who wants that? We have come a long way from the fears and admonitions of Edwards and Cotton Mather. We want hope, an answer to the darkness. A *way out*.

We want to go to Sweden with Yossarian, not to be told that it is no better there than it is on Pianosa, or in Rome. Robin Vote is shown all of the Western world, from Berlin to New York, from museums to circuses, and in the persons of Felix, Nora, and Jenny she is given the full spectrum of responses to that world. She rejects it all. O'Connor knows and understands all, and knows it to be unredeemably ugly—not just dull, but final, foul, and evil.

In *Nightwood*, there is no escape for the man who would be human; even the bleak cynical survival of a Shrike is denied him. The physical world is, as Shelley termed it, "A dome of many-coloured glass," but it is not staining any "white radiance of eternity"; it merely futilely conceals the blackness at the core. The apparitions that we call our lives are good in that we have them, but it is the most dangerous form of madness to ask for any purpose, Divine or not, behind them. There is no pattern, no history, nothing real either after or before in either historical time or the stillness of eternity, just an endless, unrelated stream of images, existing only in the moment. So Nora loses Robin when she tries to make her hers, to give a meaning to their relationship that would outlast the moment.

> Yet sometimes, going about the house, in passing each other, they would fall into an agonized embrace, looking into each other's face, their two heads in their four

hands, so strained together that the space that divided them seemed to be thrusting them apart. . . . To keep her (in Robin there was this tragic longing to be kept, knowing herself astray) Nora knew now that there was no way but death. In death Robin would belong to her.

"In passing each other," and only "sometimes," there would be contact. Two dogs sniffing each other, as they pass through life sharing the same kennel.

What people really ask O'Connor for is a way to connect the moments, a way to find the pattern that they know must be there simply because it isn't. What he gives them in return is the night, the fact of physical night as a metaphor for the real night of human isolation, the fantasy of dream as a metaphor for the failure of living. He cannot, like Shrike, tell the girl with no nose that she will find one, nor can he, like Lonelyhearts, demand suffering. He can only demand that he be left alone, and fail even in this.

He began to scream with sobbing laughter. "Talking to me—all of them—sitting on me as heavy as a truck horse—talking! Love falling buttered side down, fate falling arse up! Why doesn't anyone know when everything is over, except me? That fool Nora, holding on by her teeth, going back to find Robin! And Felix—eternity is only just long enough for a Jew! But there's someone else—who was it, damn it all—who was it? I've known everyone," he said, "everyone!" He came down upon the table with all his weight, his arms spread, his head between them, his eyes wide open and crying, staring along the table where the ash blew and fluttered with his gasping breath.

His mind exploded, the gagging bile of truth filling his mouth, he can only allow his body to be led home by a queer ex-priest. Each Christ has his own particular Paul.

William Butler Yeats, his head filled with *A Vision*, wondered what the nature of the Second Coming would be, what the "rough beast" destined to be the Messiah would really look like:

> The Second Coming! Hardly are those words out
> When a vast image of *Spiritus Mundi*
> Troubles my sight: somewhere in sands of the desert
> A shape with lion body and the head of a man,
> A gaze blank and pitiless as the sun,
> Is moving its slow thighs, while all about it
> Reel shadows of the indignant desert birds.

A bit before this passage, Yeats says, "everywhere/ The ceremony of innocence is drowned." This is the world, where O'Connor drunkenly tries to move his "slow thighs" away from the table in the café. God has finally, mercifully, let go, and allowed man to discover the truth for himself. In the world as it is, the "ceremony of innocence" *is* drowned; it exists only where Robin and the dog can chase each other, "grinning and crying," through the broken toys and crushed flowers in front of the altar, until they collapse.

All that the twentieth century has really done for man is to make it easier for him to see himself with "a gaze black and pitiless as the sun," and harder for him to find the pity he still needs so desperately. The tears of Mary have all dried up, and Christ's body has become petrified wood. People, in *Nightwood*, travel constantly and easily but they don't go to the old shrines or grottoes. Instead they go to Dr. Matthew O'Connor for their cures, and he prescribes "wrath and weeping" instead of the baths; the only relics he has for sale are empty glasses. Yeats's pitiless gaze is not

Ten Versions of America

only that of the sun; it belongs to the full moon and to the starless night as well. It is the gaze of the world when man asks it for answers. It is the original look of Robin, and the final blankness of O'Connor. It is life itself.

And life is only images, moving meaninglessly through time.

Unless you ask questions.

HAZEL MOTES

Wise Blood is as much a comic novel as *Nightwood* is. There Robin Vote opted to stay with the animals; here Enoch Emery, the boy with "wise blood, like his daddy," is rewarded by "his god" with a gorilla suit which Enoch takes from a huckster at a kiddy matinée. There Dr. O'Connor staggers, drunk, into the night, prophesying "wrath and weeping"; here Hazel Motes, self-blinded, only wants to die in a drainage ditch.

Man appears foolish because there are things he cannot

know. There is no simple solution for the complexity of his nature. So he seems to stumble through his life, assuming stances that he is sure are faultless, but, when seen in another's eyes, are merely ridiculous. He can be mimicked, humiliated, and, worst of all, simply replaced. There is always someone else to be what he imagines himself to be, someone else to wear his image, whether that image be a gorilla suit, or a white hat and an $11.98 shiny blue suit. If you're not the proper sort of prophet, there is another in the wings who will be.

Man can control neither time nor truth. He is, as the name Motes indicates, a speck of dust—of no more importance. Yet he is, or should be, able to keep trying. To push, if dumbly, against the world.

This is what Hazel Motes does.

To the world around him, Motes looks like a bizarrely dedicated preacher, with his funny clothes and intense stare. He himself does not know who he is or what his calling is. He knows only that people die, that people who live are frauds, that he hates Jesus without knowing why; and that no one, particularly himself, likes the idea of the coffin lid closing.

> He was asleep now and he dreamed he was at his father's burying again. He saw him humped over on his hands and knees in his coffin, being carried that way to the graveyard. "If I keep my can in the air," he heard the old man say, "nobody can shut nothing on me," but when they got his box to the hole, they let it drop down with a thud and his father flattened out like anybody else.

From his childhood, he knows something else:

There was already a deep black wordless conviction in him that the way to avoid Jesus was to avoid sin. He knew by the time he was twelve years old that he was going to be a preacher. Later he saw Jesus move from tree to tree in the back of his mind, a wild ragged figure motioning him to turn around and come off into the dark where he was not sure of his footing, where he might be walking on the water and not know it and then suddenly know it and drown.

Faith. But how can one have faith in the Hound of Heaven, driving you into sin so that he can save you, take you from this life to another? Or, for Hazel Motes, how can one not? He wants to be the "preacher to that church where the blind don't see and the lame don't walk and what's dead stays that way," but the only way that he can achieve it is to become the blind, the lame, and the dead himself. Like Miss Lonelyhearts, he demands the recognition of suffering, not as salvation but as an end in itself. And, like Lonelyhearts, he achieves it, with the *coup de grâce* delivered by a fat cop with a new billy stick. Deliverance. Leaving poor dumb Mrs. Flood, the landlady, talking to a corpse and looking into his dead, deep eyes.

Hazel Motes's goal is exposure of the fraudulent, and, at the same time, finding that which he cannot expose. He goes on a quest through the seedy back streets of a sick, sad Southern city. Yet the South is not important. The seediness is. Motes searches for the truth among the shills, the crippled, the dumb, and the ugly; the desperate and those who cannot even be that. He is a very strange combination of Shrike and Lonelyhearts, possessed of the sight of the one and the vision of the other. He is driven to expose the horror of the world to those who already know it and are using their knowledge and to those who would not know what to do with the truth if it were given to them. Most of all, he wants to prove to himself that the world is what he knows it to be and that he himself is, as he knows—obscene, "abominable among the filthy people."

His Church Without Christ is to be the Church of This World, his sermon that which Dr. O'Connor wanted so much to deliver in *Nightwood*. But he finds out, as did Dr. O'Connor, that when one tells the truth it is no longer a private thing, and the one who tells it, if he does not become Christ, picks up unwanted disciples; he becomes a marketable commodity and others can make money off his madness. Hoover Shoats (professionally known as Onnie Jay Holy):

> "You watch out, friend. I'm going to run you out of business. I can get my own new jesus and I can get Prophets for peanuts, you hear? Do you hear me, friend? . . . Yeah and I'll be out there doing my own preaching tomorrow night. What you need is a little competition. . . . Do you hear me, friend?"

Each new Jesus meets his disciples. God shakes hands with Uncle Sam. And The City becomes the city.

Nightwood had the world of the circus running under and through it. Its characters were clowns, aerialists, and animals; the world of *Wise Blood* is the ugly backside of the carnival, with the shills trying to hustle each other or at least exchange the fraternity handshakes of the cheaters. If Hazel Motes really wanted to escape Jesus by avoiding sin, he went to the wrong place to do it. Every character in *Wise Blood* is neck deep in sin. Stealing, whoring, killing;

the Seven Deadly Sins cavort together in a very genuine Dance of Death.

Wise Blood is a Ben Jonson comedy with the Humours full-blown and the laughs gone. There is no Lovewit in *Wise Blood*, just a cop with a new nightstick who clubs a dying man the last step of the way. But then *Wise Blood* is about America, and it is a Christian novel about a world without Christ.

To Jonson greed was a sin, but it was also a craft practiced by single-minded blatantly obvious knaves on fools just as greedy. In the end, everyone got his just desserts. To Flannery O'Connor greed was also a sin, but the end result was death, not exposure.

It is difficult to talk about greed in American society, and literally impossible to talk about good old-fashioned greed, because it is so easy to call it something else. Competitive and consuming, our always-expanding economy rewards those who make use of it. It cannot be sinful to want more if that's the whole point of being alive. Joseph Heller's Milo Minderbinder, the supreme twentieth-century con man, knew that the way to happiness lay down the *real* "yellow brick road," and followed it with far more joy than did Dorothy. The characters of *Wise Blood* are not so fortunate. They know that the dollar is the answer, but they are novitiates, either too dumb or too young to really make it. They hustle, all right, but with a desperation and an ignorance that frustrate them at every step. Like Hoover Shoats. He knows that he has to keep his eyes and ears open to catch opportunity. He was, after all, "a preacher and a radio star," but he grabs for a dollar rather than the big money and says the wrong thing to the wrong person. To Hazel Motes:

"Why, do you know who you put me in mind of when I first saw you? . . . Jesus Christ and Abraham Lincoln, friend."

Hazel's face was suddenly swamped with outrage. All the expression on it was obliterated. "You ain't true," he said in a barely audible voice.

"Friend, how can you say that?" Onnie Jay said. "Why I was on the radio for three years with a program that give real religious experiences to the whole family. Didn't you ever listen to it—called Soulsease, a quarter hour of Mood, Melody, and Mentality? I'm a real preacher, friend."

He sure was, but unfortunately Haze was the wrong congregation. To the gullible, Christ and Lincoln are magic names, offering unlimited charismatic possibility. But to Hazel Motes, for whom Christ is "a matter of life and death," charisma is much more than repugnant; it is pure sin. To the man who wants to lacerate himself, there is no magic in beauty. Hoover looks elsewhere and,

On his second night out, working with his hired Prophet and the Holy Church of Christ Without Christ, Hoover Shoats made fifteen dollars and thirty-five cents clear. The Prophet got three dollars an evening for his services and the use of his car. His name was Solace Layfield; he had consumption and a wife and six children and being a Prophet was as much work as he wanted to do.

Hoover proved that he could get "Prophets for peanuts," and in any sane carnival things would simply stop there. Hazel would have realized that he had been outhustled and moved on to another corner. But Haze refuses to play according to the rules of the world. He won't let himself be taken, and he reacts in a very direct and brutal way:

> The Prophet began to run in earnest. He tore off his shirt and unbuckled his belt and ran out of his trousers. He began grabbing for his feet as if he would take off his shoes too, but before he could get at them, the Essex knocked him flat and ran over him. Haze drove about twenty feet and stopped the car and then began to back it. He backed it over the body and then stopped and got out. The Essex stood half over the other Prophet as if it were pleased to guard what it had finally brought down. The man didn't look so much like Haze, lying on the ground on his face without his hat or suit on. A lot of blood was coming out of him and forming a puddle around his head. He was motionless all but for one finger that moved up and down in front of his face as if he were marking time with it. Haze poked his toe in his side and he wheezed for a second and then was quiet. "Two things I can't stand," Haze said, "—a man that ain't true and one that mocks what is. You shouldn't ever have tampered with me if you didn't want what you got."

A very dark, very pre-Christian prophet, who offers the dying Layfield a very bleak last rites:

> "You shut up," Haze said, leaning his head closer to hear the confession.
> "Told where his still was and got five dollars for it," the man gasped.
> "You shut up now," Haze said.
> "Jesus . . ." the man said.
> "Shut up like I told you to now," Haze said.
> "Jesus help me," the man wheezed.

117

Haze gave him a hard slap on the back and he was quiet.

No fool in a Ben Jonson comedy was ever dispatched in that way, but then Hazel Motes does not pretend to be either wise or benevolent. Enoch Emery is the one with "wise blood," who wants to be "THE young man of the future, like the ones in the insurance ads." Haze "don't want nothing but the truth!" And that truth is death—not pretty, but certain. When he disposes of his *Doppelgänger*, he does so because Solace Layfield is not Hazel Motes and yet tries to wear his skin. To get his gorilla suit, Enoch Emery must kill the man inside of it, silence the "surly voice inside the ape-suit." He knows that he is the true Gonga, and that once inside the skin, he would, like Frankenstein's monster or Mighty Joe Young, only want to do good, to use his superior strength to help those less fortunate than himself by offering them his hairy paw. He can't help it if people run away, and he is left "on the rock where they had been sitting" staring at the "uneven skyline of the city." Enoch only wanted love and friends and the man in the gorilla suit had them, shaking every hand. So why shouldn't its rightful owner, the thwarted lover, have it?

Enoch wants love, Haze truth; between them they lick the leftovers off the platter of virtue. They are both murderers. Enoch is a voyeur, Haze a masochist. They are the good people in *Wise Blood*.

Both Hazel and Enoch want a straight path to what they feel is the meaning in life. Neither one of them can stand deviations off the course once it has been set. So, when the man in the ape suit tells Enoch to go to hell, Enoch must kill the man and wear the suit himself in order to preserve its powers with proper respect. And Haze is honor-bound to expose anyone he considers to be a fraud who crosses his way, from the porter he is sure is from East-rod to the hired prophet Solace Layfield. Along the way he meets Asa Hawks, who inadvertently points out his vocation to him.

Ten years ago at a revival he had intended to blind himself and two hundred or more were there, waiting for him to do it. He had preached for an hour on the blindness of Paul, working himself up until he saw himself struck blind by a Divine flash of lightning and, with courage enough then, he had thrust his hands into the bucket of wet lime and streaked them down his face; but he hadn't been able to let any of it get into his eyes. He had been possessed of as many devils as were necessary to do it, but at that instant, they disappeared, and he saw himself standing there as he was. He fancied Jesus, Who had expelled them, was standing there too, beckoning to him; and he had fled out of the tent into the alley and disappeared.

Ever since, Hawks had taken to the streets, wearing the black glasses of the truly blind, preaching his gospel for pennies. Hazel wants two things from Hawks—to believe him and to expose him. He gets both. First he demands to know why Jesus doesn't heal Hawks if He healed others, to which Hawks replies: "He blinded Paul." Then he sneaks into Hawks's room at night and holds a match before his eyes, and "the two sets of eyes looked at each other as long as the match lasted."

At this time, Haze was already preaching the gospel of the Church Without Christ:

"I preach there are all kinds of truth, your truth and somebody else's, but behind all of them, there's only one truth and that is that there's no truth. . . . No truth behind all truths is what I and this church preach! Where you come from is gone, where you thought you were going to never was there, and where you are is no good unless you can get away from it. Where is there a place for you to be? No place."

And Haze's big discovery of Asa Hawks's fraudulence is simply summed by Sabbath Lily Hawks:

"I thought anybody would have seen what he was before that without having to strike no match. He's just a crook. He ain't even a big crook, just a little one, and when he gets tired of that, he begs on the street."

Just a little crook, and what's wrong with that? To the world, nothing; it's only a shame that Hawks couldn't have been more successful, couldn't have brought his act to television. But to Hazel Motes it is a mortal sin, knowing a lie and then selling it as the truth. "You ain't true."

But if the truth is that "there's no truth," what difference should it make what Hawks or Layfield says or does; why should one be driven away and the other killed? The fact of the matter is that to Hazel Motes there very definitely is a truth:

He said it was not right to believe anything you couldn't see or hold in your hands or test with your teeth. He said he had only a few days ago believed in blasphemy as the way to salvation, but that you couldn't even believe in that because then you were believing in something to blaspheme. As for the Jesus who was reported to have been born at Bethlehem and crucified on Calvary for man's sins, Haze said, He was too foul a notion for a sane person to carry in his head. . . .

Five miles down the highway on his journey to "the new city," a patrolman stops him and pushes his Essex off a cliff. When he finishes his three-hour walk back to the old city, he buys some quicklime and blinds himself.

"There's no other house nor no other city."

The Hound of Heaven caught him; the "ragged figure" pulled him into the trees and put pennies on his eyes. Hazel Motes wanted to talk straight to the world, to tell it that there was no meaning save in the moment, no truth save the passing of time, no morality anywhere, and that sin was imaginary. But he was carrying coals to Newcastle; the world knew that all the time.

There *is* "no other city" than the one that poor Enoch Emery looks at, his heart beating with unrequited love inside the ape suit, from his hilltop, and there is no way to escape it. Hazel Motes was mad when he tried to show the world itself, sane when he decided to stop looking at it. His mortification of the flesh is much different from that of Miss Lonelyhearts. Lonelyhearts hallucinated himself away from his own failures into an imaginary vocation. The City drove him mad, all right. It forced him to look at his own inability to love. It is warped love, not sin, that is Lonelyhearts's problem. He tries, even at the desperate end, to turn out from himself. He wants to believe in Christ as love and not as suffering. He cannot. Haze is not concerned with love; that's Enoch's province. Nor is he concerned with suffering, save for his final purification. He wants knowledge. As The City feeds Lonelyhearts's need for suffering by offering up to him a surfeit of the pathetic and deformed, so it feeds Hazel, bringing him complete corrupt worldly wisdom.

Yet while Haze and Enoch make their respective quests, the world simply goes on about its business. Enoch is openly ridiculed and Haze is either coveted or excused for his queer behavior, but, except for murder or theft, they have no effect upon the world. And, even in the murders, we don't know the effect. The bodies are simply left, like broken, discarded toys. Enoch sits on the hilltop; Hawks is supposedly on a banana boat somewhere; Lily is in a detention home; Hazel dead—but the world unchanged. The world is certainly real enough, and Haze and Enoch seem strange only because they are in such sharp focus. We don't follow the other characters with any detail; they simply appear and disappear, like the nameless and faceless grubs of *Miss Lonelyhearts*. None of them, not even Hawks or Sabbath, is given any real substance; they exist only in what they want or don't want in relation to Haze. The cheap carny atmosphere of The City comes from looking at it with clear vision, without excuses. What is real is horrible, and "What's dead stays that way." Hazel Motes's family is dead; Enoch kills the man in the ape suit; Haze kills Solace Layfield; Haze blinds and mortifies himself. Lonelyhearts was driven by his nightmare of Christ; Dr. O'Connor by his inability to be Christ; Haze by his desperate need to know that He isn't necessary.

Of the three of them, it is only Hazel who is able to scream in his soul, "*Mea culpa*." He cannot, like Hawks, try to effect an imitation of Paul, because Christ is too real to him. He blinds himself because the vision of the world and the sight of himself are unbearable.

There is a terrifying combination of Greek and Christian ethics in *Wise Blood*. There is no God the Father, only Apollo, Athena, and Jesus. If Oedipus could cry, "It was Apollo, friends, Apollo!" so Hazel Motes can know in his broken body, "It was Jesus, friends, Jesus." Oedipus offered up his body as his blessing to man, bringing with it the gift of knowledge that man should never let his pride blind him to the world and his actions in it. Hazel offers his torn corpse to Christ in a belated, unasked-for "Imitation." And this world moves on unaffected, with only the landlady, a pathetic selfish Mary Magdalene, as witness to what has actually happened.

Apollo and Athena functioned in a marvelous way in Greek thought: their manifestations were never destructive; they simply reinforced or corrected man in his thoughts and actions. But Christ had to blind Paul in order to get him to listen. When Oedipus blinded himself, he was, in effect, paying homage to Apollo, apologizing for his failure to imitate the "farsighted one," for trying to stumble off on his own, trying to control the world, but blind to its reality. Hazel Motes's blinding is also an apology, to Christ, for Haze's inability to see.

A Christian man's sight is deliberately limited, his horizons carefully limited. There simply are things that he cannot know, and if he tries to intensify his concentration on the world around him, making up in depth for what he lacks in scope, he ends up like Hazel Motes, forced into blinding himself because he cannot stand to look on the world as it is. The more carefully one looks at something, particularly if that something is another person, the uglier it becomes. There is no room in the Christian world for intense examination, unless one is able to admit that what he is looking at is not really important in and of itself; that this world is, ultimately, no more than shadow and the substance lies elsewhere. Then we can look at our world with cold and precise eyes, and choose our jobs from among the crooks and the scientists. But the poor "mad Puritans," like Dick Diver, and the Christ-haunted, like Hazel Motes, don't have that choice.

To the public Christian, in this country and in this century, Christ doesn't exist. The words are there, at the ready, but He is safely tucked away where He can't complain about blasphemy. It is easy to profess and appear publicly on Sunday, dressed for the eyes of the community, and take part in a simplified, harmless ritual. Words are said, agreed with, and forgotten. The clothes are carefully hung up and the television sets turned on. Christianity is simply something one should do on Sunday morning, but, as Wallace Stevens says, in his poem "Sunday Morning," "Why should she give her bounty to the dead?" If there is no more meaning to Christianity than the public one, why worry about it? Most people don't. There is no question of "bounty"; being a Christian is no more of a bother than being a Lion or an Elk.

But for some, no matter how simple being a church member may be, no matter how tightly Caesar bear-hugs God, there is still the notion of Christ scampering about. That is dangerous. One gets the feeling, in the company of Motes, Lonelyhearts, and Dr. O'Connor, that Paul wreaked incredible havoc on the human spirit by going out and getting himself blinded and then telling about it. To Hazel Motes, belief in Christ *is* a matter of life and death. His failure to understand demands his death; there is no choice. Just as there was no choice for Lonelyhearts save madness, or for O'Connor save oblivion. Trying to solve the paradox of killing a man who dies to save you is more than just difficult. It is impossible, unless one is ready to offer the same sacrifice. Ahab's dream is fulfilled in strange ways. On crowded, ugly, dark streets and back alleys; in saloons and sickbeds; with screams and silence; with lie compounding lie until everyman can say to himself, "You ain't true." But the dream comes true anyway and the white whale dies slowly of starvation in the murky waters of a goldfish bowl. And Jesus, whether he hangs mutely on a wall or scampers in the dark or staggers from bar to bar, is an orphan at last. He has given his message and now, politely, or with bile, asks only that he be left alone.

TOMMY
WILHELM

"When it came to concealing his troubles, Tommy Wilhelm was not less capable than the next fellow." Whatever happened to Jake Barnes and Dick Diver, as they went their various ways to the discovery or destruction of self, they traveled under their own names, had at least that claim to identity, while Miss Lonelyhearts tried to cloak his failures under the public wrap of anonymity. For the "dark nights," they thought they had a me to talk to. Not Wilhelm. He cries out for his "true soul," as Dr. Tamkin calls it, but ends with nothing—soulless and nameless as well. Tommy he knows is a fraud, a name he gave himself hoping to escape the world he was born to and make real the fairyland dream of Hollywood. But there he ended, not as Rhett Butler with his Scarlett in his arms, but a bear-like extra in kilts squeezing mute bagpipes. He is "Wilky" to his father; an unaffectionate childhood nickname carrying only disdain into middle age. "Velvel"—his grandfather called him that —he'd hoped was the real him, but the little boy's smile became ugly when his teeth came in and were short split-apart stumps, and the body that could be held comfortably, bouncing on a knee, thickened to the point where only the flab bounced and reflected hippopotamus from the mirror. If he had been bright enough, or his hands not so big and clumsy, and had gone to medical school, Wilky could have died and he could have been Dr. Wilhelm Adler, carrying pride with him and bringing luster to Adler, the title of the species.

But he wasn't, and didn't, and stays Wilky—a little shame-filled boy, reminded each morning at breakfast that his pill-taking, smoking, Coke-drinking body is no more than a shell, barely concealing, through its bulk alone, the failure that is living and growing inside. And he lives in a hotel, filled with the dying, unable to pay his bills.

The Gloriana is one of a group of hotels clustered around the faded brilliance of Stanford White's monstrous, decaying "baroque palace," the Hotel Ansonia on 74th and Broadway. Verdi Square, on 72nd Street, is now a gathering place for whores, queers, pushers, and cops. But at the time of *Seize the Day*, it was the type of place where Eleanor Roosevelt would come to speak to an audience of octogenarians, all carefully bundled and lined in rows, each in his proper and accustomed place, on the old green benches. Some of them still sit there, but now there is fear in their eyes and no one comes to talk to them. They are there because they cannot afford the luxury of the "Sun Cities." They are not "Senior Citizens"; they are simply old men and women, not retired because there was never anything for them to retire from, and the wrinkles on their faces are from the bitterness of empty lives rather than from age: dying, hate-filled animals driven to a filthy, littered ground.

When poor fictional Tommy Wilhelm lived in his fictional Gloriana, there were no "Sun Cities" to siphon off those with enough money to choose their final homes. The old seemed happy living closeted in rooms in hotels older than they were, eating in dining rooms offering the illusion of what had once been service, or in the comfortably garish convenience of new cafeterias with their beautifully arranged montages of spoiling fruit; and daily, some perfunctorily, some with deadly, greedy seriousness, they would make their way to one of the small brokerage branches in the neighborhood to watch their fortunes rise or fall on the ever-changing board. One—and particularly a middle-aged, desperate failure—could never with any certainty separate the honest old face from the fraudulent. Who had the money? The real money? And who was lying?

Take old Rappaport, for instance. According to Tamkin, Rappaport had made enough money off chickens to support two separate families with enough children to fill the phone book with Rappaports, all, like their father, quoting Teddy Roosevelt. Wilhelm doubted the old man with his Churchill-size cigars and his eyes so bad he had to have his wheat figures read to him from the board, but if, as he claimed, Teddy Roosevelt really did kick him off the beach at the Battle of San Juan Hill, then maybe the whole story was true after all. And why would anyone lie about that?

The incredible greed which dominates every page of *Seize the Day* is funny, but it is certainly not comic. The old men, from Dr. Adler through Perls and Rappaport to Tamkin, are bizarre, grotesque, almost frozen and one-dimensional in their dedication to the roles they've chosen for playing out their time; but there is the aura of malice in the air about each of them. To Wilhelm, they do not seem to want to be left alone; vampire-like, they want the blood of another to thicken their own. Wilhelm tries his damnedest to understand. He wants help—and love. He only wants his failure to be understood and forgiven, not criticized and played upon.

Wilhelm is a Jew. Even as big, blond, newly named Tommy arriving in Hollywood, he was a Jew. Even as a Rojax salesman, peddling kiddy playthings throughout "the New England territory," he was a Jew. And particularly now, in the day of *Seize the Day*, he is a Jew.

Nathanael West told his story of man, in cynical, desperate twentieth-century America, using conventional tools. America was made by the Puritans; it was their ethic of hard, humble, constant work that created, in scarcely three centuries, what passes for the model of practical, industrial efficiency among all nations. The surface of our nation, pollution aside, glistens with a radiance that, could they see it, would glaze the eyes of our Founding Fathers with the knowledge of the diligence that went into its creation. Everything they could have dreamed of is here. *Now.* From the mini-museums dedicated to their faith and hatred that we have hidden in safe quiet East Coast retreats to the wild-eyed desperation of the final pioneers trapped in California spitting oil and garbage into the ocean that stopped them from gobbling more land. We have taken everything our ancestors could have wished for. From a lovely white house in the hills above the Pacific, our President can watch the descendants of the gulls which circled around the *May-flower* try to pull themselves out of the black ooze that was a coastline, and still have time for thankful services on Sunday.

It's a little more difficult with Tommy Wilhelm. First of all, he has no Christ to model his suffering upon, and not the slightest hope of the reward of heaven if he succeeds. No real God the Father who sent His own Son to earth, only somewhere in the dim past the angry voice out of the whirl-wind telling poor, blistered Job that he is a failure because he is not God. And Wilhelm, who, if he ever thought about it, would see himself as Job, hears an angry voice himself: the voice of his father. Lonelyhearts could turn the wrath of his failure on those around him, demanding that they suffer more; Wilhelm can only, like a bad dog, carry his failure down to the breakfast table each morning to meet the condemnation of his father.

Condemnation it is.

Dr. Adler was a success and had retired proudly and comfortably to spend his last years in the only splendor he desired, the modest cleanliness of the Gloriana. No one, least of all Tommy, knows how much money he has, nor does anyone, save Tommy, care. He is a respected, dignified

"Old Gentleman." Yet, in what year did his wife die? Was it '31? Or '32. "I believe the year was closer to nineteen-thirty-four, Dad." Wilhelm knows the year, month, day, "the very hour of his mother's death." But then Dr. Adler was a very busy man, working to save lives and help his family.

Dr. Adler is not evil. He is simply selfish, in the purest sense of the word, interested in himself to the exclusion of all others and feels, quite naturally, that any sane man is of the same mind. If Tommy screams at him for love, Adler knows that he only wants money. It's Tommy's fault that he's not his father, and no one is more aware of that fact than Dr. Adler. Adler has genuinely made it in his, and America's, terms. He is both wealthy and healthy, and if he is neither altruistic nor charitable, what physician since Hippocrates has been? Such is his point of view, and if his "me-firstism" seems awesomely callous, it is, at the very least, totally realistic and completely successful.

Love, in the world of *Seize the Day*, does no one any good, and the only pity present is the ludicrous self-pity of Tommy. Reason is what one needs, if one is truly to "seize" the day, and reason is what Dr. Adler personifies, as surely as Tamkin preaches it. He has dealt with himself and his world in such a way that he has survived and holds, as he faces his son across the breakfast table, the tiny triumph of his glistening old age.

Greed and fear kill families. Dr. Adler is afraid that Tommy and Tommy's sister are ready to "bleed" him to death by taking his money. Real blood money, the money actually his blood, his children assassins, his only safety to be found among those definitely closer to death than he is himself. He feels that he is honest, as opposed to Tamkin. His medical degree is certified, his career a matter of record that anyone could look up. He merits any pleasure that he can find in his old age. Why should his children be after his money? Why should they want to know how much he has? It is his, his secret. His reward. His. And if he cannot wear it proudly as others wear their military medals, he knows in his soul that the battles he fought to win it were at least as violent and as brilliantly won as any ever fought by Alexander, Caesar, or Patton. He has worked hard, for himself, in the eyes of others, and he deserves anything he can get, and he is right, when his slovenly, failure-ridden son comes on his knees, begging, to both feel and articulate his disgust. He is right but not human. His son is, sadly, too much his opposite.

Dr. Adler knows that Tommy is a failure and that it is Tommy's own fault, and not his, but why must it follow that his failure renders him unlovable? He is, in spite of his weakness, his stupidity, and his ugliness, a human being with an existence tentative at best. If only he had money.

Tamkin explains to Wilhelm the necessity to make and to love money:

> "Money and Murder both begin with M. Machinery. Mischief."
> Wilhelm, his mind thinking for him at random, said, "What about Mercy? Milk-of-human-kindness?"
> "One fact should be clear to you by now. Money-making is aggression. That's the whole thing. The functionalistic explanation is the only one. People come to the market to kill. They say, 'I'm going to make a killing.'

It's not accidental. Only they haven't got the genuine courage to kill, and they erect a symbol of it. The Money. They make a killing by a fantasy."

The world Tamkin is describing to Wilhelm is the modern human jungle. It is a world where the dominant principle is the survival of the fittest, and the weapon, instead of the tooth and claw of the unsophisticated jungle, is the dollar. If we do not expect the tiger to have mercy on the antelope, why should we expect the successful father to have mercy on the failed, wasted son? Murder through the possession of money is not a crime. Tamkin is right; it is "killing by a fantasy," but people die nonetheless. What drives Wilhelm mad is that death by failure has such slow, agonizing pain. In order to "seize the day," one must live in the day. Wilhelm has no present, only remorse for the past and fear of the future. Tamkin's "M's"—money, murder, machinery, and mischief—all have to do with survival and success in the here and now; Wilhelm's pathetic mercy and milk-of-human-kindness are what could and should be, but aren't.

As in life, so in art, and it should be no wonder that as the incidence of suicide grows greater in twentieth-century American life we should find it reflected in our fiction, nor should it be curious that the boundary lines between murder, death by accident, and suicide have somehow or other become blurred. What we witness in *Seize the Day* is the last day in a man's life. Wilhelm, in his sobbing envy of the corpse in the coffin, is dead. We do not need to know any more; we are present at the funeral. But was it murder, suicide, or death by accident? Certainly old Dr. Adler was not so filled with malice that he actually desired his own son's death. Tommy's failure was not only an irritant but a disgrace to the old man, but he only wanted Tommy away from him and his money, not dead. All Tamkin wanted was Wilhelm's money, not his life. And Wilhelm's struggle, impotent as it is, is only to stay alive. Yet there is certainly nothing accidental about what happens to Wilhelm.

Wilhelm is an American, as surely as is any son of a Puritan minister. As such, he not only wanted but expected to succeed; it was only a matter of choosing the right career. He knew, at an early age, despite the protestations of his mother, that he was not his father, that he could never be a doctor, or a lawyer, or any other kind of "professional" man. He went to Penn State, where he distinguished himself as a big, blond, affable fraternity man. He left before the end of his sophomore year to go to Hollywood and make his fortune as an actor:

> This was typical of Wilhelm. After much thought and hesitation and debate he invariably took the course he had rejected innumerable times. Ten such decisions made up the history of his life. He had decided that it would be a bad mistake to go to Hollywood, and then he went. He had made up his mind not to marry his wife, but ran off and got married. He had resolved not to invest money with Tamkin, and then had given him a check.

Tommy's a dummy. He was born to be affable and nice, to be what he was with the Rojax Corporation, a salesman, but never, as he had expected, a vice-president. He's not a Willy Loman, losing his job because his second-rate talents faded out of existence. He simply reached his peak and then refused to recognize it. He wanted the whole of the Ameri-

137

can Dream, not just his allotted portion. So when Maurice Venice, the would-be agent, real-life pimp, whose very name carried the kiss of death in Hollywood, told him, after looking at Tommy's screen test, that there was no sense in his even trying to make it as an actor, he went anyway. He went because a door had been opened a crack and he had a peep at possible success, and once that had happened there was no one who could close it again, except Wilhelm himself.

It is impossible to tell a person his place in America. He can be forced into it, either socially or economically, but he still dreams. Little girls read movie magazines; little boys read stories of the Presidents, or Henry Ford, or John D. Rockefeller, and even though they probably know, no matter how tender the age, that the reality is beyond them, the dream never is. They are force-fed success stories, bloating up their hopes like the livers of geese. Look at Honest Abe; look at Andrew Jackson; look at Charlton Heston. And Gary, Indiana, Peoria, Illinois, and Eugene, Oregon, wipe tears from their eyes as their young burn their farmer's blue work shirts and, wearing silly-looking ties, head for the *City* to make their own Andy Hardy movies.

It still happens. Even now. This minute, there are thousands more American kids sitting in waiting rooms or trying to justify their twenty years of simple, dull, dream-filled living to the carefully honed, precisely automated personnel directors of New York, Chicago, or San Francisco than have ever thought of marching on Washington.

They are Americans—not the descendants of the original settlers, but of the unwanted, those who followed—and now they feel it is their turn to get a piece of the pie that their fathers and grandfathers picked the fruit to fill. Most of them get it, not as much as they wanted, but enough to buy themselves bits of respectability: cars, color TVs, "own homes." They get enough of the Dream to keep them from hallucinating.

Not Tommy Wilhelm. The American Dream and his desperate, foolish lust for it have brought him, both bloody and bowed, to the point, as he ends the day of *Seize the Day*, of ultimate humiliation: the recognition that incapable Wilky was the real him all the time, and that Oh, God! it would be so much better if Wilky were dead. It was in California that Wilhelm changed his name from Wilhelm Adler to Tommy Wilhelm, and it is to that time that he traces the beginnings of his "downfall."

"Lucky Dick" Diver was king of his world, ruler of the beach and the café. Fitzgerald very carefully established Diver's world and the brilliance of his appearance before he took us inside him. Bellow takes exactly the opposite approach:

> When it came to concealing his troubles, Tommy Wilhelm was not less capable than the next fellow. So at least he thought, and there was a certain amount of evidence to back him up. He had once been an actor—no, not quite, an extra—and he knew what acting should be. Also, he was smoking a cigar, and when a man is smoking a cigar, wearing a hat, he has an advantage; it is harder to find out how he feels. He came from the twenty-third floor down to the lobby on the mezzanine to collect his mail before breakfast, and he believed—he hoped—that he looked passably well: doing all right. It was a matter of sheer hope, because there was not much that he could add to his present effort.

139

No brilliance here. Not even the slightest bit of security. Diver, as we discover in the course of *Tender Is the Night,* is concealing troubles when we first see him in his jockey cap on the beach, but he is concealing them with the consummate skills of a great actor; he is much more capable "than the next fellow." Tommy, once "an extra," smoking his cigar, wearing his hat, only hopes that he looks "passably well." The "advantage" he hopes for is merely to pass as an ordinary man: "doing all right." "Doing all right" is an American phrase and it is horrible. What Tommy Wilhelm has within him is a cry of anguish, and he has been conditioned to be terrified of uttering it; he can only hope that he will not scream. Training. It is better to burn your guts out with false guilt than to show a tear on your face.

"Doing all right" means, one hopes, "Better than you are," or, at worst, "As well as you are." But in the American Dream there simply isn't room for everyone to "do all right." Yet it's a sin not to. So what does the failure do? He lies, or tries; he puts on an act that he hopes will cover him until he makes It; hides his shaking hands in his jacket pockets; takes pills he calls "vitamins" to control his hands so that he can light his cigars and take the tremor from his voice. "Doing all right" means money, and money, to Americans like Tommy Wilhelm, means the possibility of freedom from fear—financial security, which is the only type of security that we are taught to respect. If you don't have money, you're a prisoner, trying to find temporary escape in trashy paperbacks or straight gin in small glasses in front of TV sets. Yet even there Wilhelm is caught by his dad, as he sits on the edge of his unmade bed, panting with his stolen bit of joy as the Giants win, bringing only more disgust to his father, standing there, silent, his nostrils distorted by the stench of dirty socks and shorts. Wilhelm knows it. There is nothing in the world that he would like more than to please his father by being a success; he doesn't want to be hated. He doesn't want to be a failure.

In the "day" of *Seize the Day*, we witness his final attempt; his last grasp at the Dream. In the morning, Wilhelm's existence is a "matter of sheer hope." By the evening, that hope is dead. It decomposes bit by bit. First it is a hope that his appearance is good enough to carry him down the elevator, through the mail pickup in the mezzanine, and in to the breakfast table; a hope that his father will show some genuine, human, being-to-being love for him; a hope that Tamkin is not a fraud and that he will not lose his last bit of money on the stock market; then a hope that his dad will carry his rent through one last week; then a hope that his estranged wife will not try to milk him for money that he does not have. Each individual hope dies with increasing agony until, finally, he finds himself staring down at a dead stranger in an open coffin.

But first the elevator doors open and we are confronted full-front with overgrown, red-faced Tommy Wilhelm, replete with hat and cigar. He has already done everything he can; as Bellow says, " . . . there was not much he could add to his present effort." We are asked in only for the end, as though we came in late for a performance of *Othello* and saw only the last act. Tommy's kids, his dog, and his poor, dear, Catholic Olive—those closest to him—appear only as names; a litany of once-known joys invoked in the agony of a death throe. We know that they are not dead and that he can still see them, but on this day they are no longer his;

all that is left of them for him are their names: Olive, Paul, Tommy, Scissors. They are the "good" memories, hurting even more than the bad ones, haunting him as he races from breakfast to Tamkin, to the market, to lunch, to the market, after Tamkin, and to the funeral.

It is really so simple. In his heart—or his "real soul," as Tamkin would call it—all Wilhelm truly desires is that which all sane men should desire: a home, a woman to love, children, and a faithful dog. Yet, unlike Odysseus, who knows throughout his entire twenty-year absence that he will get home again, Tommy knows that that dream is gone. He tries to delude himself into believing that it is not all his fault, that it would have been possible if only people had understood him and helped him, but at the end there is no escaping the fact that he is Wilky and not Odysseus. Odysseus was not bothered by money; Wilhelm is obsessed with it. Everywhere he turns, he sees, like an insane, crippled Ayn Rand hero, the dollar sign that he cannot quite reach. His wife, Margaret, demands money; the Gloriana demands money; his father refuses him money; Tamkin takes money away from him; and at the end Wilhelm simply has no money left. Of course, it's the "pretender soul" that's destroyed in this way, but how does one, as Wilhelm learns so painfully, ever separate one soul from the other?

It would be a blessing if Tommy were a true complainer, but he isn't. He tries, like the real American failure that he is, to hold it in. Like any terrified child, he can only say, "Dad . . . " But his "Dad" is not only his father; it is his world, and, most of all, it is himself.

Wilhelm has one day to recoup the failures of forty-some years, and only the urge, none of the abilities, to accomplish it. This we know from the beginning of the book, and Bellow never lets us forget it. Tommy's indecisions are really unimportant. Everything has already happened. In the main, our world has not worked out, and we feel, as does Wilhelm in his deepest heart, that somehow or other it is our fault. In the purest, and maybe the truest, sense of the American Dream, it is our fault. After all, God isn't after us if we really do the job, make the money, and support the family. Happiness isn't His concern, and anyway who's happy in the long run? It is security, not joy, that's important; money, not the answers to painful cries, that marks the man.

What Tommy Wilhelm demands is not himself, but the reason why he can't be himself; love, even if he can't quite understand it, not money. But he has been conditioned to feel that self and then love come through money and the success that it brings with it, that the self that he presents to others is the important self and that presentation is much more *important* than reality.

"That's the way the world ends. Not with a bang but a whimper." Poor Tommy can't even build a fence or shoot a rifle to protect himself from the savages; he can only ask them for mercy, and everybody knows that savages never give mercy, whether they wear loinclothes or Phi Beta Kappa keys. It's a marvelous reversal of the old frontier society laws—the family in the log cabin has won, and now its only business is the killing off of the unfit members. From Athens to Sparta is a very short trip, and America has made it in a very short time. The Wilhelms, and many of the rest of us, simply have to recognize that some journeys are too rigorous.

What made Wilhelm quit his secure, if unspectacular, job with the Rojax Corporation? He was a failure as an actor. Maurice Venice was right—he didn't have the stuff; and he probably shouldn't have married the woman he did, but quitting his job was a different mistake from the others. Hollywood was a dream, the hope of a big, dumb kid; the marriage was the result of a mistake many men make, confusing lust with the ideal of love; the Rojax decision involved something no one encountering Tommy Wilhelm in the lobby of the Gloriana would ever imagine he possessed—pride. Wilhelm once had it, and it was all caught up in his notion of what it meant to be a man.

Being a man can be confusing to a twentieth-century American. The words "responsibility" and "success" seem to lose their respective identities and become one. How can one "meet his responsibilities" if he's broke? Tamkin's right; Seize the day! Make a killing! Paranoia is not a sickness; it is seeing the world as it is, so long as you use it for profit. There are people looking at you from behind your back, waiting for you to make your fatal mistake. You have to use every bit of peripheral vision you've got. Then, although you've no guarantee that you'll make it, you'll at least have the knowledge that you've done your best. But Wilhelm's back is too thick. He can't turn his head fast enough to see the gremlins who are plotting his defeat. He quit his job at Rojax because he thought he was better than he was. He was never cut out for even the modest duties of a vice-president; his simple-minded charm made him a good salesman, but that was it. It wasn't the nepotism Wilhelm imagined that kept him from the job he wanted, it was his own limitations. He could have been responsible; never, in his terms, a success.

Until he looks into the coffin, Wilhelm doesn't really want to die; he just doesn't want to be a man. He has tried, and that should be enough. Now that he has failed, it is his father's duty to take care of him. It would be nice if Wilhelm's father were a little kinder, if he showed some evidence of love or understanding toward his son, but, cruel or not, there is no law that says a man must support a son into his forties. Aeneas carried the aged Anchises; Tommy asks the opposite and he is turned down.

NEIL KLUGMAN

Many things contribute to success in America: pride, hope, the will to live, what we call "stick-to-it-iveness." In *Seize the Day*, Saul Bellow strips those qualities away from Tommy Wilhelm one by one until, finally, he weeps with envy over an unknown corpse. It is pathetic, but it is also very bitterly real. The world is an unfair, unsympathetic, unlovely jungle, and in it man is ultimately alone—owed debts by no one for his own existence. Poor Tommy Wilhelm finds himself his own debtors' prison in the middle of

America's terminal ward, and then screams, "Help me, love me!" Only the corpse has no good advice to offer.

Tommy Wilhelm isn't the only one who finds himself looking at corpses. Neil Klugman, in Philip Roth's *Good-bye, Columbus*:

> Instead of grabbing a cab immediately, I walked down the street and out towards the Harvard Yard which I had never seen before. I entered one of the gates and then headed out along a path, under the tired autumn foliage and the dark sky. I wanted to be alone, in the dark; not because I wanted to think about anything, but rather because, for just a while, I wanted to think about nothing. I walked clear across the Yard and up a little hill and then I was standing in front of the Lamont Library, which, Brenda had once told me, had Patimkin Sinks in its rest rooms. From the light of the lamp on the path behind me I could see my reflection in the glass front of the building. Inside, it was dark and there were no students to be seen, no librarians. Suddenly, I wanted to set down my suitcase and pick up a rock and heave it right through the glass, but of course I didn't. I simply looked at myself in the mirror the light made of the window. I was only that substance, I thought, those limbs, that face that I saw in front of me. I looked, but the outside of me gave up little information about the inside of me. I wished I could scoot around to the other side of the window, faster than light or sound or Herb Clark on Homecoming Day, to get behind that image and catch whatever it was that looked through those eyes. What was it inside me that had turned pursuit and clutching into love, and then turned it inside out again? What was it that had turned winning into losing, and losing—who knows—into winning? I was sure I had loved Brenda, though standing there, I knew I couldn't any longer. And I knew it would be a long while before

I made love to anyone the way I had made love to her. With anyone else, could I summon up such a passion? Whatever spawned my love for her, had that spawned such lust too? If she had only been slightly *not* Brenda . . . but then would I have loved her? I looked hard at the image of me, at that darkening of the glass, and then my gaze pushed through it, over the cool floor, to a broken wall of books, imperfectly shelved.

I did not look very much longer, but took a train that got me into Newark just as the sun was rising on the first day of the Jewish New Year. I was back in plenty of time for work.

The mirror should be no more than that; it shows our blemishes, our aging, and getting behind it is no more than an act of self-admiration, a way of saying, "Well, you're not as bad as you look." But Neil transforms the mirror. "Mirror, mirror on the wall, who's the fairest . . . Snow White!" Nonsense! Let's go further. Herb Clark or not, the mirror has to justify, make "those limbs, that face" right in whatever they do or show. Put Tommy Wilhelm next to Neil in front of that glass; watch Tommy fidget, hands brushing his clothes, eyes darting from side to side, desperate to turn and run. Watch Neil stare, silent, thirty seconds to purge and justify the hurt inflicted by touching another, then time to check the watch and catch the train, and in the shadows behind them, gaunt, gray, and stern, the specter of Jonathan Edwards, one arm outstretched to draw yet one more member to the ranks of the elect. Which would he choose?

In the full giddiness of ego, Neil Klugman is very careful to point out the grossness of everyone with whom he comes in contact, from his aunt's Velveeta cheese and

Brenda's father's toilets, to her brother's pathetic, sentimental hang-up with Ohio State University. But behind all the idiocies of the world he encounters is the final, brutal stupidity of Neil's vision of himself. When Gilley, in Malamud's *A New Life,* asks S. Levin why he is doing the insane thing of throwing over his career to run off with Gilley's homely, pushy, flat-chested wife and their kids, Levin answers, in a marvelous wild, romantic outcry, "Because I can, you son of a bitch." What Neil is saying to himself into his window-mirror is, "I can't, you son of a bitch." And he's right. If Levin looks at the world and accepts the fact that his new life is not at all what he thought it would be, Neil looks at the world and loves himself for denying any possibility of a new life at all. He shifts his gaze from his supposed introspection to the "broken wall of books, imperfectly shelved," and goes back home again.

What difference should "new lives" make anyway? Short Hills is no better or worse than Newark, Dairy Queens are just as bad as Cuban heels, and the public pools in Newark surely no more polluted than the oceanfront pools of Miami Beach; and if the beaches of the Caribbean are better than Coney Island, it is only that fewer of us have enough money to go to them. But Neil's ego is saying something else; it is saying that "I" am better than the world around me. Nothing need change so long as I am me; that is not true. A man who views his world with total contempt and continues to live in it is a suicide.

Hatred is not enough, and contempt considerably less. If there is any value left in the world as it is, it lies in gaining self-knowledge and in learning how to love—or, rather, in letting oneself love, not in trying to find out why you can't love, and then walking away content in the knowledge.

People can't afford to observe each other from a distance, either critically or sympathetically, yet for Neil it seems that it is equally dangerous to get too close. Neil looks at Leo Patimkin, pathetic light-bulb salesman, and feels glad that he isn't him; he sleeps with Brenda Patimkin, lovely social-climbing Radcliffe girl, and pretends that he loves her. Old Leo is unaffected, as "Old Leo"s always are; Neil is only an ear into which to lodge the regrets of a lifetime of frustration, but Brenda, maybe, wanted something else.

There is humor in *Goodbye, Columbus,* but it is bitter, not sympathetic. The book is not comic. There is no triumph of the human spirit, however insignificant, anywhere in it. There is malice, there is coldness, and there is cuteness. In fact, Neil's major characteristic is his cuteness. The following exchange between Neil and Brenda about Brenda's "nose job":

> "I'm afraid of my nose. I had it bobbed."
> "What?"
> "I had my nose fixed."
> "What was the matter with it?"
> "It was bumpy."
> "A lot?"
> "No," she said. "I was pretty. Now I'm prettier. My brother's having his fixed in the fall."
> "Does he want to be prettier?"
> She didn't answer and walked ahead of me again.
> "I don't mean to sound facetious. I mean why's he doing it?"

"He *wants* to . . . unless he becomes a gym teacher
. . . but he won't," she said. "We all look like my
father."

"Is he having his fixed?"

Neil is serious, and he is, from the very beginning of the
book, a cold fish to surpass all cold fishes.

Dick Diver told Rosemary Hoyt that "the manner remains intact for some time after the morale cracks," and
proceeded to demonstrate, through personal example, the
cracking of the manner. In *Goodbye, Columbus*, there is no
evidence that there ever was any morale at all, and the manner of Neil is no more than self-conscious ridicule from a
position of imagined superiority.

> Slowly, softly, the Ohio State University band begins
> the Alma Mater, and then the bells chime that last hour.
> Soft, very soft, for it is spring.
> There was goose flesh on Ron's veiny arms as the
> Voice continued. "We offer ourselves to you then,
> world, and come at you in search of Life. And to you,
> Ohio State, to you Columbus, we say thank you, thank
> you and goodbye. We will miss you, in the fall, in the
> winter, in the spring, but some day we shall return. Till
> then, goodbye, Ohio State, goodbye red and white,
> goodbye, Columbus . . . goodbye, Columbus . . . good-
> bye. . . ."
> Ron's eyes were closed. The band was upending its
> last truckload of nostalgia, and I tiptoed from the room,
> in step with the 2163 members of the Class of '57.
> I closed my door, but then opened it and looked back
> at Ron: he was still humming on his bed. Thee! I
> thought, my brother-in-law!

Of course, the record's silly and Ron obviously isn't
Neil's type, but who is? Lonelyhearts was a hater, but, like

any true hater, his hatred manifested itself in total disgust, not in mere disdain, and the creature whom Lonelyhearts hated most was himself. Not that Neil Klugman should be a mad, Christ-haunted, Puritan failure, but his hatred is so prissy that he ends up sounding campy, self-adulating. "Thee!" The reason for hatred, at least in a sensitive human being, has to do with the condition of humanity, not with the way people look and talk. If you're disgusted by the man with spinach in his teeth, you're really disgusted by the fact that you were trained to turn away from him. Anybody can ridicule a harelip.

Yet that's all Neil does, harelip after harelip; from Mrs. Patimkin's sister Molly, "a tiny buxom hen whose ankles swelled and ringed her shoes," to her brother Marty Kreiger, "an immense man, as many stomachs as he had chins, and already, at fifty-five, with as many heart attacks as chins and stomachs combined." What's the reason for all this ridicule? Maybe Neil Klugman is the end product of all that America has been building for, the cynic who reveals through his nasty condescension the essential desperate frailty and the sad dying beauty of other human beings. Because the human beings in *Goodbye, Columbus* are marvelously human, and terribly frail.

Only Neil is pure and rational; only Neil sees the stupidity and ugliness of those around him. The others go on humdrumming through their lives, bitter at times, limited, basically futureless, but not knowing any of it. Neil knows.

But that's all Neil has. He sees and loathes the emptiness of others' lives, but doesn't realize that he has no core himself. He is an ignorant, introverted modern version of Shakespeare's Thersites, a scurrilous railer, but one who rails silently, making no attempt to expose the fools or improve the world. Neil has no alternatives to offer, nothing to put in the place of Patimkin Sinks, nothing better than either Newark or Short Hills.

> . . . I simply looked at myself in the mirror the light made of the window. I was only that substance, I thought, those limbs, that face that I saw in front of me. I looked, but the outside of me gave up little information about the inside of me. . . .

One of the things we learn in reading *Goodbye, Columbus* is that there is precious "little information" inside of Neil to be given up. We are able to answer the questions he puts to himself at the end of the book. They all have to do with the reasons for and the nature of his love for Brenda. And they can all be answered with one simple statement: he didn't. He wanted her as a possession, something to show off: his very own Jewish princess. But, as a lover, he is the categorical opposite of Humbert Humbert and miles away from S. Levin.

Everyone in *Goodbye, Columbus* is carnal and acquisitive, and Neil knows this. He is even ready to accept his own acquisitiveness. He just wants to know which prize will fulfill his need, which prize is God: Is it "Gold dinnerware, sporting-goods trees, nectarines, garbage disposals, bumpless noses, Patimkin Sink, Bonwit Teller," or a combination of all of them, capped off by the prize of Brenda? Just point it out and Neil will accept it.

It's hardly a religious quest, but it's not meant to be. God is not dead, in a kind of insane Transcendentalism, He is present in every object man makes to make himself more comfortable or more important in his fellows' eyes. God is

greed and the object of life is to get from Newark to Short
Hills and then make sure that your old neighbors don't
make the same move. But once one has achieved that goal,
what then? Those among us who achieve the earthly Paradise of a Short Hills, Shaker Heights, or, even better, the
new walled-in, guarded, self-destructing suburbs continue
to make money, to want to make money, because it's what
we were trained to do and what we do better than our fellows. We can't stop. So the endless procession of gadgets,
from improved swimming pools to perfected faces and
odorless bodies, priced to fit any budget, the best for the
wealthiest, and so on down the line. Acquire and Discard;
Invent and Make Obsolete. If God is not inherent in the
very process itself, then Neil Klugman is quite right to ask
where *He* is.

Consumer products are meant to be consumed. And
perfected American Puritan morality means simply produce so that we may buy, so that we may produce more—
ad infinitum. It matters not that the characters of *Goodbye,
Columbus* are American Jews; they are as caught up in the
realization of the American Dream as any of Lonelyhearts's
letter writers. Neil's observations, nasty and impotent as
they are, are basically true. It is strange to see trees passing
themselves off as oaks when actually they are "sporting-
goods trees," trees with, "beneath their branches, like fruit
dropped from their limbs, . . . two irons, a golf ball, a tennis can, a baseball bat, a basketball, a first-baseman's glove,
and what was apparently a riding crop." And equally
strange to find, in an obscure corner of a Short Hills base-
ment, an old refrigerator, a reminder of "the Patimkin roots
in Newark," filled almost to overflowing with unwashed

fruit of every conceivable kind. It is a Pleasure Island that would drive Pinnochio crazy, a world where man is really doing business with nature, and a world where he is sure that he is winning, that he has everything under control. And if it is a world that would bring Daniel Boone helpless to his knees, it would surely haze over Ben Franklin's famous eyeglasses with sheer joy. Nature can't complain, and so long as we wash off the fruit that we refrigerate before we eat it, we won't, as Julie Patimkin says, "get diarrhea."

There really is no reason why Neil, obscure, skinny, introverted Gulliver that he is, should not say, "Oh Patimkin! Fruit grew in their refrigerator and sporting goods dropped from their trees!" It is a miracle, and if God hath not wrought it, then surely man is God, and there is nothing that he cannot either conquer, perfect, or buy.

But man hates man. Whether it's Neil's icy condescension or Mr. Patimkin's overcapitalized forgiveness at the discovery of Brenda's diaphragm, each man believes that he, and he alone, is right; he may feel sorry for or hate his fellows, but he knows in his heart that they are not his equals. As Mr. Patimkin phrases it in talking to Grossman, of "Grossman and Son, Paper Box": "Shit on that. You're not the only one in town, my good friend." No one is "the only one in town" save the person speaking. And, no doubt, after his chewing out at the hands of Patimkin, Grossman will call up someone whose job it is to service him and give him his just deserts in turn.

Yet among the Patimkins and the Grossmans, much of the nastiness is just "good fun," part of the game of American business. Patimkin can even wink at Neil as he says, "Shit on that," to Grossman. In Neil's observations there is no fun, no friendly understanding of the game: Patimkin would go and weep profusely at Grossman's funeral; at anyone's funeral, whether parents or Brenda, Neil would sit cynically, observing the eccentricities of the grievers and wondering why he didn't feel worse, why he couldn't cry, ever, honestly. Neil not only knows that other people are not his equals; he despises them for the fact.

"Hard work never killed anybody." "A man works hard he's got something." Mr. Patimkin to Neil Klugman. He's right, and Neil knows it, but he can't accept it. Neil really knows that hard work is "right"; he only hates the people who do it, because he thinks that the work they are doing is the wrong work. As Brenda says:

> "Neil, what are you talking about! You're the one who doesn't understand. You're the one who from the very beginning was accusing me of things? Remember? Isn't it so? Why don't you have your eyes fixed? Why don't you have this fixed, that fixed? As if it were my fault that I *could* have them fixed."

Neil *is* "the one" who doesn't understand. He blames people for their minor successes, and their trivial pleasures, as though, somehow, they were depriving him of something by trying to believe that they were having joy out of living.

Swift had his Gulliver take fantastic voyages, accidentally, to unreal countries populated by giants, midgets, or horses, to show the horror not only of man's manners, but the real basic ugliness of man himself. Roth takes his Gulliver into the realest of countries in order to show the same thing, and Neil learns even less about himself than did the original Gulliver. When Swift ends *Gulliver's Travels,* with Gulliver's pronouncement that men had better stay

159

away from each other until they realize what foul creatures they are, he is really saying the same thing that Roth is saying when he has Neil turn away from the window-mirror: man is shit not because of the things he has or the way he looks, but at the very core of his being.

Brenda is simply asking Neil if it is her fault that she is the person she is, and, more importantly, why he wanted her in the first place. He doesn't know. "If she had only been slightly *not* Brenda." It's an experiment that Neil tries, as much of an experiment as that of the Wright brothers at Kitty Hawk. He wanted to see if he could achieve Short Hills, with Brenda and the Patimkins and all that went with them. Yet at the same time, in the purest spirit of the pioneers, he knew that to really achieve what he wanted he would have to conquer Short Hills. When the Pilgrims landed and the Indians were kind to them, they were amazed, but they also knew that if they were to survive, the Indians would have to be defended against or, better yet, eliminated. This from the very beginning. Neil, when he first arrives in Short Hills, is amazed at the largesse and the generosity of the Patimkins. After his first Patimkin dinner, in spite of the cynicism of his comments about the conversation, he is able to say very simply: "I am full." But it is a strange land; there is too much there—twenty-three unopened bottles of Jack Daniels, as just one for-instance—and obviously the natives don't know how to make proper use of the riches in their hands. Had Neil been born a century earlier, he, not Ron Patimkin, would have shot buffalo from train-car windows for sport.

Neil is a Puritan.

And the Puritans are the greediest people of all. They

simply do not know what to do with their greed. Neil would like to take a drink from one of the unopened Jack Daniels bottles, but "you had to break a label to get a drink," and Neil was afraid of being caught. The early settlers learned how to build forts as they moved West, so that they would never be caught by the natives. Neil's fort, although it is internal and not nearly so impressive as those the English and the early-American pioneers built, is a fort nonetheless, and Neil has made sure that he will never be caught. And, as the early Americans hunted down the enemy, the Indian, and rendered him impotent, so Neil hunts down the enemy, Brenda, and renders her impotent. The only difference is the choice of weapons: the pioneers used the rifle; Neil uses the diaphragm.

Once the enemy is destroyed, the Puritan is, at least momentarily, freed.

> . . . I looked hard at the image of me, at that darkening of the glass, and then my gaze pushed through it, over the cool floor, to a broken wall of books, imperfectly shelved.
>
> I did not look very much longer, but took a train that got me into Newark just as the sun was rising on the first day of the Jewish New Year. I was back in plenty of time for work.

"Plenty of time for work." Which, of course, is what Neil wanted all the time. No Puritan wants love, only God, and He means work. Short Hills can never be taken by the first sortie.

Tommy Wilhelm's anguish marked him as a failure and —beaten, dumb creature—there was no way he could scrape it off. Eyes blurred, head bowed, he stumbled from mistake to mistake, his pockets filled with the last wharf rats grubbing among the bits of tobacco and loose pills for the final penny before it was time to desert the sinking, bloated, red-faced ship. But it's just back to work for Neil. Better luck next time.

Ben Franklin would have made Neil a full partner had he lived to see how Neil "used venery."

YOSSARIAN AND
FRIENDS

In *Tender Is the Night*, we have at least the illusion of sunlight. The Divers play out their charades amidst the glittering façades of Europe's beautiful places. Lonelyhearts plays out his life at night; in the daytime he is sick. The only relief from Delehanty's or the apartments of Shrike or the Doyles is the country with Betty, and its health is strangely poisonous. Good food, good sex, and sun upset Lonelyhearts rather than heal him. Yet in both *Tender Is the Night* and *Miss Lonelyhearts* we are meant to believe in the world we see, be it the Riviera or the sooty, rank city at night. It is supposed to be the real world, and the people in it are meant to be believed in as real people. Lonelyhearts or the "clean old man" are to be seen as real as either Diver or Abe North. Joseph Heller introduces *Catch-22* with the following brief apologia.

> The island of Pianosa lies in the Mediterranean Sea eight miles south of Elba. It is very small and obviously could not accommodate all of the actions described. Like the setting of this novel, the characters, too, are fictitious.

The Riviera, Paris, Switzerland, and Rome of *Tender Is the Night* are immense. We see the characters as tiny dots, until we get to know them, and even then we see them as much smaller than their world. We can always pull the camera back and put them into perspective. The New York City of *Miss Lonelyhearts* is equally overwhelming; Lonelyhearts cannot stand to look at the crippled Doyle in sunlight; he can only grasp his hand under the table in the darkness of Delehanty's.

In *Catch-22*, the world is not overwhelming; it is too small. It is man that is overwhelming. It is his fault that everything is destroyed. The sun shines in brilliance not on the playlet of the Divers but on the severed legs of Kid Sampson standing briefly on the raft, "joined by strings somehow at the bloody truncated hips," before falling awfully, awkwardly into the water. Legs severed because somehow the usual, low-flying pranks of McWatt got upset, either by a gust of wind or a "minor miscalculation," and the laughing, showing-off Kid got sawed in two by the propeller of McWatt's plane, and McWatt flew his plane, covered with Sampson's still fresh innards, into the side of a mountain.

The night is no better. It is the dark night of Yossarian wandering the conquered, bombed-out streets of Rome, AWOL, looking for Nately's whore's kid sister, who was kicked out of the whorehouse that had been her home for most of her twelve years (a real twelve-year-old virgin, not one of Milo's thirty-four-year-old ones) by the MPs with clubs and morality on their side; kicked out *sans* coat to make her way on the streets in winter. It is the night that Yossarian does not so much see as feel, hear, and touch. The noise of beating, whether of dog, child, or drunken whore, or of teeth crunching under his feet as a young soldier sits sobbing with a stinking handkerchief jammed into his bloody mouth, while the cops tell a group of soldiers trying to immobilize a soldier having an epileptic fit to hold on to him, that he's "under arrest."

Cold, wet, and dark. The worst sound that echoes over Yossarian's night in the Eternal City is the sound of barbaric human laughter, the laughter of those in control, capped, finally, by the laugh that Aarfy must have laughed when, after he had raped a chambermaid and then held her until after curfew when he felt he could toss her with impunity out of the window to her death, the MPs come to arrest Yossarian for being AWOL and apologize to Aarfy for disturbing him.

Catch-22 is not a funny book.

Heller's vision has been compared to that of the Marx Brothers. The Marx Brothers are consumed, if not, like the rest of the characters in one of their movies, by the image of self or position, at least by what they want, whether it be woman or merely laughter. We see their wisdom in that they see the world as foolish, an ideal place for greedy men, which they are, and in the fact that although they are judged as ridiculous by the supposedly powerful people surrounding them, they emerge triumphant at the end—or, at least, safe. Their safety is never in doubt; like Jerry the mouse when chased by Tom the cat, we know from the very first of a Marx Brothers movie that they are never going to be in any real danger. People don't die in a Tom and Jerry cartoon or a Marx Brothers movie, because in the make-believe world of fools and knaves there is no such thing as death. There is only exposure.

In the real world of fools and knaves, there is no possible way to expose enough fools to stop the dying. And Joseph Heller is talking about the real world, where the fact of death, always inescapable, is made even more horrifying in that men are asked to die for something that, simply translated, means other men's ambitions and greed. It is as though Groucho were shot to advance the career of the floorwalker. Groucho isn't; but Snowden is, and he spills his secret out in the back of the plane:

> Snowden was wounded inside his flak suit. Yossarian ripped open the snaps of Snowden's flak suit and heard himself scream wildly as Snowden's insides slithered down to the floor in a soggy pile and just kept dripping out. . . . He felt goose pimples clacking all over him as he gazed down despondently at the grim secret Snowden had spilled all over the messy floor. It was easy to read the message in his entrails. Man was matter, that was Snowden's secret.

168

Tiresias examined the entrails of birds to foretell the future. Yossarian looks at Snowden's guts and sees the present. It is the instant in the individual's life that is important in Heller's vision, because there might not be another one. Nobody runs an ordered universe and those with the ambition to run one are out to kill you. So the sane man concentrates on the only thing he has: trying to stay alive. As Yossarian says to Major Danby:

> "I'm not running *away* from my responsibilities. I'm running *to* them. There's nothing negative about running away to save my life."

Man's only responsibility is to his own hide. What Danby means by responsibility is doing what someone else wants you to in order to maintain the status quo of society. But Yossarian knows that this is Catch-22 thinking and he has learned, by the end of the book, how to beat it.

Throughout the book, various characters, from Doc Daneeka to Yossarian himself, attempt definitions of Catch-22. But it is the old woman in the ruined, cleaned-out Rome whorehouse who finally succeeds. Yossarian arrives after the MPs have chased the girls out into the street and smashed up the furniture, and the following exchange takes place:

> "There must have been a reason," Yossarian persisted, pounding his fist into his hand. "They couldn't just barge in here and chase everyone out."
> "No reason," wailed the old woman. "No reason."
> "What right did they have?"
> "Catch-22."
> "*What?*" Yossarian froze in his tracks with fear and

alarm and felt his whole body begin to tingle. *"What did you say?"*

"Catch-22," the old woman repeated, rocking her head up and down. "Catch-22. Catch-22 says they have a right to do anything we can't stop them from doing."

The setting of *Catch-22* is the war of living. With one simple sentence, the old woman cuts through the bureaucratic jungle of explanations that are not explanations but justifications which merely confuse, to put her finger and our eyes on the exact nature of the ruling principle of American society. Catch-22: "They have a right to do anything we can't stop them from doing." It makes no difference whether the "they" refers to the MPs, or to Colonel Cathcart, or to Milo Minderbinder, or to the Germans or the Americans, or to men in peace or in war. "They" is organized man; "we" is the individual. When Yossarian, later in that frightening night in Rome, hears a man cry "Help! Police!" while he is surrounded by them, he cannot help but wonder if the cry is not really a warning.

Man is alone, really alone. Only if he makes a "deal," as Yossarian almost does, is he accepted and safe, and even if he makes his particular deal, the safety has only the illusion of permanence, for the "powers that be" are not always the same. One must be able, like Milo Minderbinder, to deal with anyone at anytime; to sense the change in the breeze which tells one to shift allegiances.

There is much of Shrike's philosophy in *Catch-22*, but there is no longer the need to articulate it, and, instead of driving sensitive men mad, it makes them sane. Recognizing the world for what it is heals Yossarian, pulls him out of his hospital bed, and puts him to flight, making him realize that funny, apple-cheeked Orr was right all the time and that his plodding diligence was simply a method of getting out and protecting himself. As Shrike knew the world, so does Yossarian, but as Shrike tried to preach the gospel, Yossarian knows that the only gospel he has is the very limited and delicate flesh of his own body and that it is not a matter of preaching but one of preservation.

The world remains the same, its ugliness and corruption only accentuated by the war. The opportunists triumph and nothing succeeds like excess. The American Dream runs rampant toward fulfillment during wartime, simply and brutally because so many die that there is more room for the carefully self-interested who would never be so naïve as to take chances with their lives. There are enough believers in causes and would-be heroes to satisfy the public at home.

The seemingly carefree and wild, like McWatt and Kid Sampson, are pure fools, because they lack even the sense to worry. Beyond their foolishness with its disastrous results lie the two avenues of self-interest: the self-aggrandizement of the Cathcarts and the Korns, and the interest in self as entity of Orr and Yossarian. The two are vastly different.

In a young frontier society, man tries to advance himself as a means of protection. The more land he has, the safer he is. He works and acquires not so much to impress his neighbors as to insulate himself and his family against them. But as a society becomes more sophisticated, the need to possess for protection becomes corrupted; instead of worrying about his neighbors seeing him, man begins to hope that they will see him, and the need for power to protect himself becomes the need for power to present himself. He looks out rather than in, at his neighbors rather than at himself, and begins to care more for what they have than for what is his. A man like Cathcart or Korn can say, in all apparent honesty, "Do this for your country," when they really mean "Do this for me." Man is taught to use words in a ritualistic sense rather than in a real one and to believe in the power of the abstract behind them. "Programmed" is the word we use now, in the age of computers; we are programmed to believe in things beyond us—history, ethical principles, religious dogma—that will give us at least the lip-service justification for acting the way we do. But lurking in the shadows behind the justifications remains the idea of the Puritan ethic or the American Dream as it came to be translated into reality. If we work hard under God, for our fellow man, for self-protection, it is one thing; but if God is dead, as he surely is in total war, and we are working against our fellow man, and self-protection means merely making as big a profit as is possible, it is another, and we need a different vocabulary with which to talk about it. The idea of the American Dream is a wonderful one, a beautiful Utopian notion, and one can almost believe in it, almost envision a land where there really is room for everybody to achieve what he wants. Where everyone can have refrigerators like the Patimkins.

Unfortunately, what the Dream leaves out is greed and envy; man wants what his fellow man has, be it possessions or position.

Yossarian, in *Catch-22*, is the good king, lord, or house-holder from Jonson, Molière, or Shakespeare; he sees what is wrong, the corruption that greed and envy have brought in their wake, but he can do nothing save run away. The neat comic exposure that Jonson used is no longer possible, and the man who knows that there is something wrong also knows that it would mean death to say anything about it, because the Tartuffes or the Faces have become Milo Minderbinder and the people with the old power of the king or the lord are the Cathcarts of the world. Everything, in short, has been reversed. Taking just *The Alchemist* as an example, Lovewit, the right-thinking master of the house, has been deposed and Sir Epicure Mammon rules in his place, his grotesque appetites constantly fed by the seemingly sycophantic but always profiting Face, while Yossarian-Lovewit wanders the perimeter, filled with knowledge of what they are doing to his property but more filled with fear because the Mammon-Cathcarts of the world kill those who get in their way. And—at least in *Catch-22*—there is no way of changing things; the reversal is complete.

In the world of the hustler, there is no such thing as permanence, or possession. One must be constantly on his toes, alert to the fact that his neighbor wants what he has and that to survive he must act first. This attitude is the basis of war, but in Heller's vision it is much more. It is the world as It is. The frontier principle of self-protection has found fulfillment in the more complicated society of the twentieth century as the principle of self-aggrandizement, and Daniel Boone has been metamorphosed into Milo Minderbinder.

In *Tender Is the Night*, Fitzgerald has Dick Diver say to Abe North and Rosemary Hoyt the following, about the First World War:

> "This took religion and years of plenty and tremendous sureties and the exact relation that existed between the classes. The Russians and Italians weren't any good on this front. You had to have a whole-souled sentimental equipment going back further than you could remember. You had to remember Christmas, and postcards of the Crown Prince and his fiancée, and little cafés in Valence and beer gardens in Unter den Linden and weddings at the mairie, and going to the Derby, and your Grandfather's whiskers. . . . Why, this was a love battle—there was a century of middle-class love spent here. This was the last love battle. . . . All my beautiful lovely safe world blew itself up here with a great gust of high explosive love."

Fitzgerald saw the First World War as the end of a way of life, spiritually as well as physically. You had to have been safe, with the sureties of "a century of middle-class love" behind you. This "love" should not be seen as in any way either romantic or personal. It is a love best translated as gratitude, the type of love we mean when we talk of "love of country" or "love of God." Soldiers fought as a way of saying thank you. Fitzgerald also means that it was the first and last war fought between equals, both socially and economically, with no real visible object; a war fought, at least in the eyes of the soldiers doing the fighting and the dying, as a bizarre expression of gratitude to Mother, God, and Country for the "plenty" of their lives: a very warped *"dulce et decorum est."* But the soldiers really believed it, at least at the first.

The war of *Catch-22* is not the First World War; it is the Second, and there is no shock and no sadness in it. The world that appeared as a melancholy confirmation to Fitzgerald is old hat to Heller.

Yossarian is a lover; the first sentence of the novel is, "It was love at first sight." He wants to love, whether it be the chaplain, Nurse Duckett, Luciana, or even Major Major. And his is not the love which is gratitude that Fitzgerald saw in World War I. It is personal, not social: romantic, not religious. He wants contact with another, which makes him appear insane to those around him, particularly to those who recognize and fear his intelligence, like Milo, Cathcart, and Korn. They know that Yossarian is intelligent, because he is capable of upsetting their plans. What bothers them is that he doesn't seem to want what they want, that he is not trying to con others, that he is honest, doesn't lie, and doesn't want to be like them.

Be like them. The Dreedles are jealous of the Peckems, and the Cathcarts of the Korns; it really makes little difference what names you use, for everyone covets what the other has, save for the outcasts. The last, dumb Boy Scouts. So it is that Major Major and the chaplain scare each other from a distance, forcing the chaplain to hide in the brush and Major Major to race in a panic for the safety of his office, where, when he is in, his orderly has strict instructions never to admit anyone. It is a world where sensitive men, like deer, are frightened by the sight of a human figure, where the only safety is to be found separated from other men.

This is the lesson Yossarian, the lover, learns over and over again. In the hands of another, his gifts, whether of mind or body, are used only for that other's gain. Only Orr and Luciana give to him, the one a fireplace and the other her body, and then both disappear, leaving him doubting them until it is too late to catch them.

Throughout the book, Yossarian and Milo are contrasted. Yossarian is self-interested, but in his self-interest is the interest in life. He asks nothing of others for himself, except his own safety. Milo wants the world. He believes in things, in what Lonelyhearts would call "a world of doorknobs," in self-fulfillment through possession. He is the personification of the American Dream gone wild. Success has nothing to do with soul. In fact, there is no such thing as soul; there are only the outer wrappings of money and position. And, back to Ben Jonson again, the real successes of the world of *Catch-22*, like ex-P.F.C. Wintergreen and Lieutenant Milo Minderbinder, have no real power in their titles. Those with powerful words before their names, the Generals, Colonels, and Majors, are interested in horseshoes, parades, and hiding from work, or, like General Dreedle, in voluptuous young nurses with which to torment their sons-in-law. Yet Wintergreen, second in power only to Milo, is a mail-room clerk; Wintergreen has power over communications; he is able to promote, demote, expose, or conceal simply by what he does with the mail, holding, forwarding, or disposing of letters. It is an awesome power in a world dependent on the written word to determine the success or failure of a man or an idea. Milo controls through men's stomachs. He is given freedom because the officers eat well and, at the same time, feel that they are getting a "good deal." Learn the lesson. You don't need a title if those who have them are, or feel they are, dependent on you. The servant is in fact the master, taking care of his superior while reaping a nice profit himself.

When Yossarian, at the end of the book, is trying to decide whether to run away, or be court-martialed, or take the "deal" that has been offered to him, he finds out that Milo, to whom he was going to turn to go over Colonel Cathcart's head, has taken Cathcart in as a vice-president with the promise of a good job for him after the war, and that Wintergreen, the alternative power to Milo, has merged with him. It has come to pass and the fools have merged with the knaves. No one listens to the voice of reason. They don't want to; to them it's not rational; to Cathcart, Yossarian sounds like Don Quixote. Corruption and stupidity are not chastised; they win, driving sanity out, alone, to the frontier, thinking only of self-protection.

America has become the enemy against which sanity protected itself, and the sanity of Yossarian and Orr can only manifest itself in trying to protect the life it has against the world in which it lives. The sane mind is left without a vocabulary. All its words are used already, and their meanings corrupted: "good" means money; "success" means the ability to fool others; "brave" means dead; "sincerely" means nothing. We are back at the very beginning again, all our fears realized, all our hopes dead. The quirk in man's nature that makes him want—rather than, as the Greeks hoped so many years ago, want to know—rules the world of *Catch-22*, as surely as Big Brother rules the world of George Orwell's *1984*. And there is an incredible, honest, non-sentimental sadness as Yossarian does the only thing he can at the end of the book: he jumps for his life, leaving Danby and the cowed, naïve chaplain behind him as the ragtag representatives of reason. We should not shout for joy at Yossarian's escape; rather we should weep at the death of the world he hoped was possible.

Beneath its savagery, *Catch-22* is about the world that might have been. When Yossarian looks around him at the misery and madness, he thinks that it is not only terrible but unnecessary as well. He is not a freak; he is an individual, thinking in his own terms and not according to a formula handed to him by his society. What Milo really does is to follow the precepts of his society, adding his personal, distinctive touch to make the recipe work. He is the world that is, the result of education, training, and practice brought to complete fruition. He is even able to tolerate Yossarian, because he knows that Yossarian can never harm him. A Cathcart may be nervous or even frightened by Yossarian's presence, but then Cathcart has his position to worry about. He wants advancement in rank, more prestige. Milo only wants more of what he already has, and he has such supreme confidence in his own abilities that no one is a threat to him. Like the Wright brothers, Thomas Edison, or Henry Ford, the realized American Dream is his for the taking; which, of course, he does.

In talking about *Catch-22*, it is easy to stress the role of Milo Minderbinder, just as it is easy to stress the Yahoos in their filth and ugliness in *Gulliver's Travels*. That the world, and particularly America, is money-grubbing and spiritless, we know, and Milo is merely a grotesque parody of John D. Rockefeller or the Two Swabbies. But *Catch-22* is more than Milo or Wintergreen or Cathcart. It is Major Major, Orr, the chaplain, and, most of all, Yossarian. In Major Major and the chaplain, there is a sadness that almost becomes cloying: Major Major, for instance, is destroyed simply because of the parental practical joke of his name and the terrible, inescapable fact that he looks like Henry Fonda, while the chaplain, an Anabaptist, is bounced back and forth like a well-meaning, impotent, ping-pong ball, even terrified of his assistant, the atheistic Corporal Whitcomb. There is no real power in either of them, just a sentimental goodness to balance the satiric hysteria of Cathcart and Korn.

If anyone should have understood Orr, it was Yossarian. Yet he didn't until the very end. In fact, Yossarian thought Orr was stupid. But Orr, who stuffed his cheeks with apples —or, if he couldn't find any, with horse chestnuts—so that he would look apple-cheeked, and who would work for hours on the tiny mechanism of a valve, was far from stupid. Walking around with apples in your cheeks sounds ridiculous. But as Yossarian comes to realize, if one wants to look apple-cheeked, what better, more rational way to do it? The sanity masked as craziness of Orr is manifest in that he does things until he has them perfected, as Yossarian sees and says to Danby:

> "Danby, Orr planned it that way. Don't you understand—he planned it that way from the beginning. He even practiced getting shot down. He rehearsed for it on every mission he flew. And I wouldn't go with him! Oh, why wouldn't I listen?"

Orr was rehearsing his escape, and he achieved it, sailing a rubber life raft from Pianosa to the coast of Sweden. He makes it out because everyone thought he was stupid and therefore harmless, because no one gave a thought to what might be going on inside his head. They just looked at his apple cheeks, buck teeth, and "look of stupid innocence," and let him through.

Genuine comedy is not an American form. If we look back on the beginnings of writing in this country, we find a literature whose primary function was control. We have never really moved away from that attitude. Even now, with the entire continent conquered and settled, the enemy (the Indian) safely destroyed or imprisoned, we still feel the need to sing and to hear the praises of "our" way of life, and to be terrified at the mere existence of another one. It is difficult to sing of the spirit in America and have it belong to only one man.

The comic does precisely this. There is no national consciousness in comedy, just as there is none in tragedy. Comedy is a game that man must win, not to further himself or to set an example for others, but in order to stay alive. In America, we look at literature in the same manner as our ancestors looked at the Bible, as a source of moral precepts by which, through explication and translation, we can guide our behavior. Instead of being something that we experience, literature is something that we learn from and we must approach a book trying to ferret out the nuggets of moral wisdom.

This country is concerned with the morality of example, not the morality of experience that is the morality of literature. We are not meant to imitate Ahab, Huck Finn, Lonelyhearts, or Dick Diver. We are meant to observe them, to learn about them, primarily an individual, special truth, not a universal, eternal verity. An attitude of moral example takes both the joy and the terror out of literature, because it takes the life out of it.

As much as we talk about the rights and freedoms of the individual in America, we are trained to respond as a group, with what we call "our national consciousness," and although this is most evident in war, it is with us all the time and, like all the elements of life in America, it can be traced back to the first settlers. As William Carlos Williams says, in *In the American Grain*:

> Their [the first New England settlers'] courage, had they been gifted with a full knowledge of the New World they had hit upon, could not have stood against the mass of the wilderness; it took the form, then, for the mysterious processes of their implantation here, of a doctrinaire religion, a form, that is to say, fixed—but small. For the great task God had destined them to perform, they were clipped in mind, stripped to the physical necessities. They could not afford to allow their senses to wander any more than they could allow a member of their company to wander from the precinct of the church.

"They could not afford to allow" says about as much as can be said of the basic principle behind "the American character." "The pursuit of happiness" does not mean joy abounding, it means profit and pleasure within bounds; life can be beautiful so long as it is regulated.

Comedy and tragedy refuse to recognize regulations. Nothing is as important as individual fulfillment, and no one or no thing can tell an individual how to find it. The one thing that real comedy or tragedy can "teach" an American is that there is something wrong with the ethical basis of his society. This is why we hear comic novels like Vladimir Nabokov's *Lolita* or Chester Himes's *Pinktoes* called un-American. They are. But then so is *Moby Dick*, or *Walden,* or, until the very end, *Huckleberry Finn.* Any book is if it sings the individual spirit at the expense of the group image. This is also why, when we get a genuine comic novel, we prefer to call it satiric, to emphasize the ironic unreality rather than the comic reality. It is safer to have a good laugh over the foolishness of Colonel Cathcart, or the completely unbelievable success of Milo, than it is to realize the comic truth that Yossarian embodies.

"*They're* trying to kill *me*" means precisely that—not us, me—and "they" means everybody, inside the society as well as out.

HUMBERT HUMBERT

"Lo-lee-ta"
Humbert Humbert.
"Lo-lee-ta."

A naïf. Living his life in one dimension while the rest of the world spins wildly around him in vastly different ones. Joseph Heller's Yossarian lives in his own special world, but he is aware of the existence of another, very very dangerous one. He knows that his life depends on the knowledge that everybody else is out to kill him. He sees the world with the clear, cold eyes of the sane; what his fellows call his pananoia is simply reasoned judgment. But Humbert wears blinders. He sees only what he thinks is in front of him, is wrong, and then proceeds to imagine what is going on to either side and behind him. Yet, through his incredible misjudgments, he reveals not only his own foolishness, but the malice and ugliness of the world as well.

"Lo-lee-ta."

> This then is my story. I have reread it. It has bits of marrow sticking to it, and blood, and beautiful bright-green flies. At this or that twist of it I feel my slippery self eluding me, gliding into deeper and darker waters than I care to probe. I have camouflaged what I could so as not to hurt people. And I have toyed with many pseudonyms for myself before I hit on a particularly apt one. There are in my notes "Otto Otto" and "Mesmer Mesmer" and "Lambert Lambert," but for some reason I think my choice expresses the nastiness best.

> Humbert Humbert.

This is mid-America, recalled from Humbert and Lolita's madcap rush trying to find the anonymity he desired so much:

> Now and then, in the vastness of those plains, huge trees would advance toward us to cluster self-consciously by the roadside and provide a bit of humanitarian shade above a picnic table, with sun flecks, flattened paper cups, samaras and discarded ice-cream sticks littering the brown ground. A great user of roadside facilities, my unfastidious Lo would be charmed by toilet signs—Guys-Gals, John-Jane, Jack-Jill and even

Buck's-Doe's; while lost in an artist's dream, I would stare at the honest brightness of the gasoline paraphernalia against the splendid green of oaks, or at a distant hill scrambling out—scarred but still untamed—from the wilderness of agriculture that was trying to swallow it.

"Artist's dream" aside, the reality of this scene is a far cry from the one Lewis and Clark or Marcus and Narcissa Whitman saw. Yet it is what all of them would have desired, could they have lived to see it. Not Thoreau; he would stand aghast could he see the hot-dog stands, parking lots, and giant water slides dwarfing his beloved Walden Pond. But Lewis and Clark and the Whitmans and the others like them wanted to bring civilization, as they knew it, to the continent they crossed and, automatically, owned. In their hearts, they, could they have envisioned them, would have desired nothing more than the "roadside facilities" their descendants achieved.

There was no malice in the first explorers of America, nor was there any in the first white men who landed and settled in cold, dark New England. They simply wanted whatever comforts that they had grown to feel were theirs by right. And not only the same, but better. They wanted to make the land better, more livable; not to destroy it, merely to improve it. And, in the land that was to become America, there was vast—almost unbelievably vast—room for improvements: land to be cultivated and planted with foreign crops; land to be cleared of its trees for houses which could be later cleared for better, bigger houses and the buildings to service the people who lived in the houses. This land *is* our land. We have no respect for it as being separate from us. It is literally ours, as surely as are our hands and feet; and, as such, we must properly clothe it, make it as comfortable as possible for us. Make it "work." The land, as Lewis and Clark saw it, was filled with possibilities, but it didn't work. It was wanted, all right, but not in its original state. It had to be made to function, to become a responsible member of the community. This, from generation to generation, we have accomplished; we have taught the land we live on, like a dog or a disobedient child, its place, and it has, to the best of its abilities, responded. It holds us, uncomplaining in the main, throughout our respective lives and welcomes our children with their own peculiar improvements. So we hope.

It's wonderful that Humbert is a foreigner. He sees our country with eyes fresher than any American's; eyes as virginal as Lewis's and Clark's, yet without their hope and greed. He sees America as it is, not as, one hopes, it will become. And he marvels at it, as, through his eyes, do we. Very few of us know, or ever will know, our country as does Humbert Humbert.

Humbert, desperately covert as lover, blatantly overt as "father," travels over the entire filled underbelly of our country.

We passed and re-passed through the whole gamut of American roadside restaurants, from the lowly Eat with its deer head (dark trace of long tear at inner canthus), "humorous" picture post cards of the posterior "Kurort" type, impaled guest checks, life savers, sunglasses, adman visions of celestial sundaes, one half of a chocolate cake under glass, and several horribly experienced flies zigzagging over the sticky sugar-pour on the ignoble counter; and all the way to the expensive places with the subdued lights, preposterously poor table linen, inept waiters (ex-convicts or college boys), the roan back of a screen actress, the sable eyebrows of her male of the moment, and an orchestra of zoot-suiters with trumpets.

Lolita is a travel book of a most unique sort. We are given a detailed description of America from two completely contradictory points of view: that of the guilty, worldly, disdainful Humbert and that of the alternately bored and bedazzled, constantly consuming Lolita. Bizarre as it seems to say, they are the perfect father-daughter as they see the sights, meet the people, and eat the food of their journey: Humbert hoping for education and the appreciation of beauty in his lover and—albeit illegally—ward; and "grim Lo," when told that a child, in some magnolia garden in some Southern state, will "walk starry-eyed and reverently through this foretaste of Heaven, drinking in beauty that can influence a life," saying, simply, "Not mine," and sitting with "the fillings of two Sunday papers." Dolores Haze knows what's important, and that's comic books, bubble gum, and the movies. Day after day, in town after town, she suffers through the sightseeing in order to sit entranced, munching popcorn and permitting the pawing of Humbert's desperate hands, watching the heroes and heroines whose private lives she had read about, so jealously, that very afternoon as "Dad" tried to point out the intricacies of a fish hatchery.

"Between a Hamburger and a Humburger, she would—invariably, with icy precision—plump for the former."

Lolita, out of bed, is everybody's pre-teen, pure American girl, while Humbert describes himself:

I was born in 1910, in Paris. My father was a gentle, easy-going person, a salad of racial genes: a Swiss citizen, of mixed French and Austrian descent, with a dash of the Danube in his veins. I am going to pass around in a minute some lovely, glossy-blue picture-postcards. He owned a luxurious hotel on the Riviera. His father and two grandfathers had sold wine, jewels and silk, respectively. At thirty he married an English girl, daughter of Jerome Dunn, the alpinist, and granddaughter of two Dorset parsons, experts in obscure subjects—paleopedology and Aeolian harps, respectively.

Add an English day school, a lycée in Lyon, college in *both* London and Paris, and the cumulative result should be the ideal person for America to try its Berlitz French on. After all, Humbert is built as we are, or think we are: he is a "melting pot" of all of Western Europe; knowing him should be the same as taking the definitive course in Western Civilization. He is what we might have been had our ancestors stayed where they were.

He is a pervert.

Humbert's not alone in his perversion. The worst pervert in the book has a biography that reads like this:

Quilty, Clare, American dramatist. Born in Ocean City, N.J., 1911. Educated at Columbia University. Started on a commercial career but turned to playwriting. Author of *The Little Nymph, The Lady Who Loved Lightning* (in collaboration with Vivian Darkbloom), *Dark Age, The Strange Mushroom, Fatherly Love*, and others. His many plays for children are notable. *Little Nymph* (1940) traveled 14,000 miles and played 280 performances on the road during the winter before ending in New York. Hobbies: fast cars, photography, pets.

Dear Cue. Ask Dolly Schiller (née Haze), as does Humbert, what forms Cue's art actually took.

> "Oh, weird, filthy, fancy things. I mean, he had two girls and two boys, and three or four men, and the idea was for all of us to tangle in the nude while an old woman took movie pictures."

So much for Rosemary Hoyt and *Daddy's Girl*. Nabokov has finished the trip that Scott Fitzgerald started us on. Lovely young Rosemary was adorable in the realization of her mother's dreams for her movie career, as was our own real-life Shirley Temple, but in spite of all the fan magazines, poor Lolita couldn't bring herself to *"souffler"* for the camera. She loved Quilty, but she still knew right from wrong.

Young America and Old Europe travel the continent together, followed by mocking, lascivious Cue, as happy in his perversion as Humbert is guilty in his and Lolita unconcerned in hers. And in their travels we see the beauty and filth of America, the strange combination brought about by man living in, and "owning" his world. Humbert is painfully right when he concludes his memoir, addressing Lolita:

> But while the blood still throbs through my writing hand, you are still as much part of blessed matter as I am, and I can still talk to you from here to Alaska. Be true to your Dick. Do not let other fellows touch you. Do not talk to strangers. I hope you will love your baby. I hope it will be a boy. That husband of yours, I hope, will always treat you well, because otherwise my specter shall come at him, like black smoke, like a demented giant, and pull him apart nerve by nerve. And do not pity C.Q. One had to choose between him and

H.H., and one wanted H.H. to exist at least a couple of months longer, so as to have him make you live in the minds of later generations. I am thinking of aurochs and angels, the secret of durable pigments, prophetic sonnets, the refuge of art. And this is the only immortality you and I may share, my Lolita.

The father, the jealous lover, and the artist are all mixed together in Humbert, as they are in all men. "Blessed matter" is what we are, and our lives, nasty though they may be, are things of beauty as well, worthy of the immortality of art. If *Lolita* is a novel about perversion, it is not a perverse book. And if the world we live in is a banal, filthy corrupted one, it is also the one in which we hear, as does Humbert, after retching at the side of a lonely mountain road, "the melody of children at play" coming to us from the valley below.

The music of existence is the theme of *Lolita*, and at the end of the concert it turns out to be lovely music indeed. Humbert says, listening to the noises of the children in the valley:

> I stood listening to that musical vibration from my lofty slope, to those flashes of separate cries with a kind of demure murmur for background, and then I knew that the hopelessly poignant thing was not Lolita's absence from my side, but the absence of her voice from that concord.

Humbert, the man-child, hopelessly confused in his roles, totally unable to grasp Wordsworth's "philosophic mind," knowing only that something is wrong, that something is missing from the world.

Bumbler though he is, Humbert is not to be pitied. His

eyes and ears and even his very ganglia yearn only for beauty. His perversion is not so much his as it is his world's. Lolita is a grecian urn brought to life, with all the corruption that life brings to art, and Humbert is unable to maintain the proper aesthetic distance. He wants to touch his "lovely Lo" with every part of his body, his every sense. It is delusion and even madness, of course, because his Lo is not really "lovely," and certainly not his; she is not even Cue's, or Dick's, but strictly her own. Like every man's desire, she refuses to fulfill, maintaining her own, irritating, disgusting selfhood in spite of her creator's wishes; the monster always laughs at Frankenstein. Humbert, the fool, is a poet who creates the wrong thing, the real world, and then tries to scan it as one would a sonnet. It's a fault, but it's not a sin, to want more than you can have and be unable to recognize it. And Humbert, in spite of his sadness and his cynicism, loves his small, stolen pleasures.

Lolita is his Frigid Princess, named, in a limp attempt at humor, after a soft-ice-cream stand: frigid, but still a Princess; unsatisfying, but still totally desirable. Humbert can't help himself; he is a human being with an artist's soul and the hoofs of the Devil. He even feels the need to attempt a sentence on himself: "Had I come before myself, I would have given Humbert at least thirty-five years for rape, and dismissed the rest of the charges." Killing Quilty was not a crime, sloppy as it was, but the seduced seducer deserves at least thirty-five years in jail. Everybody must pay, somewhere along the line, for the luxury of living, of being "blessed matter."

So Lolita died bringing forth a stillborn daughter and Humbert died of a coronary before coming to trial. Humbert's final testament is one of hope; he does not want to die, at least not right away. Thirty-five years in jail is punishment enough, and, for his Lo, he wishes happiness with her husband and her—he hopes—boy baby.

Even these meager hopes are vain. Man is matter; he can hope for nothing beyond his present moment. This is the story Humbert, without really knowing it, tells us. He tells it because he does not know what will happen; tells it, really, only to his Lolita and to himself. *Lolita* is a love poem, as personal and hopeful and sad a one as any ever written. The foreword is not merely informative; in retrospect it casts the black pall of the future over the past and present that are the substance of the book, helping to point out to us that love and hope, however demented or perverse they may appear to be, are really all we have, and we have them only now. Dr. Tamkin was right, it is crucial to "seize the day."

Humbert and Lolita, each in his or her different way, lived in the present, sometimes blindly, sometimes with clear sight, and, disregarding guilt and distaste, they took their pleasures.

Time after time, Humbert is confronted by the fact that Lolita does not love him, and finally is confronted by the fact that their whole time together was really a monstrous joke on him, but he never stops loving her. Even sitting in her tacky little house in Coalmont, looking at her pregnant body, "hopelessly worn at seventeen," he still loves her; loves her, in fact, more than ever.

But when Humbert, after one last desperate plea, sits sobbing brokenly, his Dolly says:

"You should understand. Let me get you some more beer. Oh, don't cry, I'm so sorry I cheated so much, but that's the way things are."

"That's the way things are." Lolita has grown up, has gone the way of American womanhood. From the vulgar sentimentality of Dolores Haze, she has reached the crass drabness of Dolly Schiller. She loved Clare Quilty, from far before Humbert entered her life, from the time she was ten and Quilty had pulled her onto his lap and kissed her at her mother's club. And she still loved him. Humbert, she guessed, had been "a good father." But it was Cue, not Humbert, and not Dick, who had really mattered, and he had thrown her out for refusing to be in his "movie pictures." Yet, sitting in her barely furnished living room, facing elegant, fading Humbert, with poor, dull Dick for a husband, she is able to say, and believe, that "this world was just one gag after another."

Of course it is. But would Humbert, or would we, continue to live in it if we really knew it? Because the final gag has a very bad punch line, and not very many people want to believe that their lives are nothing more than "funny." In another book, *Laughter in the Dark*, Nabokov has a scene where his accidentally blinded hero is mocked to his face by the girl he loves and her lover, both naked and silent. Humbert, too, is blind to the joke being played on him, but, unlike the hero of *Laughter in the Dark*, when he understands it in its full horror, he continues to believe; to love, if anything, with more intensity.

Humbert, the lover of beauty, is confronted fullface by the end result of all the ugliness of the real world, by the true Lolita, and he finds himself loving it more than he ever did his imaginary one. All his dreams are gone; his perfect, eternal nymphet has become a young, lower-middle-class housewife; the slangy, shallow-minded Americanisms of her childhood speech have become the mature clichés of semi-illiterate adult speech: her husband says "guess" all the time, and her final words to Humbert are "Good by-aye!" Humbert, the jaded European, witnesses the twentieth-century realization of the American Dream, where the gift of forty-five hundred dollars brings out the cry, "At this rate we'll be millionaires next!" delivered to a dog.

"Let me get you some more beer." "Stop crying, please." "No, honey, no." "That's the way things are." When Humbert, Prince Charming, makes his final proposal to his pregnant, homely Dolores, asking her to leave Dick and come with him to "live happily ever after," she can only think and say, "You mean you will give us that money only if I go with you to a motel. Is that what you mean?" What else could she think? In a world where everything is bought and paid for and nothing given, what else could the loved one think of the lover?

If his last plea is the pure, anguished one of love, all that has gone before has not been, and Dolly Schiller has grown to know full well that the world is no place for either purity or love. It's a hard lesson for a little girl to learn, but the guys who write the movie magazines are liars, at best. And those who read and believe them pay dearly for the death of their dreams: they realize that the unreachable is not only that, it isn't even there.

Humbert never read them, he never really watched the movies he took Lo to, he never really ate the popcorn or the soft ice cream, he never really consumed America, so how could one expect his dreams to be shattered? He is an observer, watching America, in the form of Lolita, consume its Dream until there is no more left. But his own dream remains inviolate, there to the last romantic hope. He is an unrepentant Don Quixote, and when he sees the reality of his Dulcinea, he loves her all the more. The world is as it is, and we are as we are. We can destroy the land, but not change each other.

Lolita grows to realize that love is not real in this world, Humbert to realize that it is the only thing that is real. Lolita grows to accept reality, Humbert to adore it.

Humbert's adoration of the real Lolita is the reason he must kill Quilty. To quote Humbert's own poem, which he makes Quilty read aloud before he shoots him:

> Because you took advantage of my inner
> essential innocence
> because you cheated me—
> Because you cheated me of my redemption
> because you took
> her at the age when lads
> play with erector sets
> a little downy girl still wearing poppies
> still eating popcorn in the colored gloam
> where tawny Indians took paid croppers
> because you stole her
> from her wax-browed and dignified protector
> spitting into his heavy-lidded eye
> ripping his flavid toga and at dawn
> leaving the hog to roll upon his new discomfort
> the awfulness of love and violets
> remorse despair while you
> took a dull doll to pieces

and threw its head away
because of all you did
because of all I did not
you have to die.

"You/ took a dull doll to pieces/ and threw its head away." Humbert kills as much for his poor "dull Doll," as for himself; not for the Lolita of his dreams but for plain Dolly Schiller, heartbroken by one pervert, youth wasted by another, sitting drably in a shack in Coalmont, made pregnant by a stupid man. He kills Cue because, between the two of them, they had made a little girl meet the real world that was her destiny too soon. Humbert really loved his Lo, Quilty only himself. Humbert's right, his "inner/ essential innocence" was surely taken advantage of, but not only by Cue. Humbert was "cheated" because he was naïve in a world where only the coldly calculating can be successful perverts. To match Quilty's memorable collection of pornography, he had only a few white anklets and an assortment of old bobby pins. Humbert was a pervert because he liked what Nicole Diver would refer to as "ickle durls" as bed partners, because he liked to park his car outside grade schools at quitting time; but Humbert was not a pervert because he loved in a world where loving is foolish if not mad, where real love is reel love, make-believe on a big screen; he was not a pervert because, with his "innocence" laid wide open and the soot and ashes of every illusion he ever had spread upon it, he looks with wide, tear-filled eyes at the world and worships it.

Of course, he was crazy.

The "hog" who was forced to face "the awfulness of love and violets/ remorse despair" was right to kill Quilty, because Cue was the *real* Humbert Humbert, the *real* pervert, who played out his deviations with as much cold, pleasureless precision as Humbert did his with rich, frustrated love. When you force Ariel to look into the mirror and see Caliban's face, he is bound to smash the mirror before he kills himself. Quilty is all that Humbert had imagined himself to be, a fully realized living obscenity, and it was him Humbert's Lo had loved. His mocking cynicism, not Humbert's earnest passion, pleased her; to Dolores Haze, he was not only "a great guy" and "full of fun" but "a genius," not at all like Humbert or Lo.

Humbert fancied himself a man of the world, felt guilt at his worldliness corrupting Lolita, but in the agonizing, awkward killing of Quilty, the final meeting was between two Humberts, the man on the movie screen and the real self. What Humbert, in his pride and his guilt, imagined himself to be, Quilty really was, in both perversion and worldliness, not a "genius" but certainly real.

American literature is filled with the agonies and aberrations of both the spirit and the mind, as men try to come to terms with themselves and their world. Ours is the realest country in the world, just as it is the most imaginary: the West Side of Chicago looking at Lake Shore Drive and dreaming. Bring us your sick, your poor, your hungry, and we'll show them people who aren't.

Little Dolores Haze dreamed only of being a starlet until she discovered that all movies, color or not, were not Doris Day comedies. But, like any sane native-born American, when her dream was gone she took whatever modest things she could from the real world. Of course she didn't love Dick; he was "a lamb," but that was about it, and—and this is what Humbert, the purist, couldn't understand—*it's* all right. She was not a lover. She had a childish dream of love and glamour, and when it proved no more than that, she accepted the fact.

Humbert Humbert had a dream, too—a place in the mountains with his child-bride and a whole "litter of Lolitas," but when his dream was shattered he reacted in a much different manner from Lo. It wasn't that he wouldn't accept it; he did that all right. It's that if it were to be shattered—a wrong—something had to make up for it—a right.

Humbert's more than a "foreigner"; he's downright un-American. He wanted to settle on the frontier with his bride and hack a life for them from the wilderness, but those days are no longer a part of America, and Quilty, despite his hysterical babbling, is very close to the truth when he says: "You are either Australian, or a German refugee. Must you talk to me? This is a Gentile's house, you know."

"This" is a Gentile's house and Humbert, with his visions of "Brave New Worlds," doesn't belong here. It's not Old Europe that's so upsetting about Humbert; it's all his nonsense about New America.

Clare Quilty is the quintessential American, and not only won't the damned foreigner leave him alone, he kills him. We all should.

But it's the naïve, twentieth-century frontiersman who actually does it. And does it with none of the neatness of Shane, the pure avenging-angel ideal of our American Western. As Humbert, after a brief, futile struggle with Quilty, describes the two of them: "Both of us were panting as the cowman and the sheepman never do after their battle." He simply shoots Quilty, with his pathetic little

"Chum," until enough bullets randomly enter his body to kill him. But old, fully realized America falls nonetheless, mortally wounded by the avenger of its corrupted, perverted, completely futile Dream, by a remnant of the old, dark, frustrated Europe that created it in the first place as the last stand of its hopes. Hum and Chum, in one last bumbling move, make the final protest against the world as it is as opposed to what it should be, and the more one reads it, the more the humor fades and one finds himself cheering Humbert on as much as one ever cheered for any imaginable Shane. It is, in short, lovely.

If only Dolores Haze could have seen the movie.

A NOTE ON THE TYPE

The text of this book was set on the Linotype in Janson, a recutting made direct from type cast from matrices long thought to have been made by the Dutchman Anton Janson, who was a practicing type founder in Leipzig during the years 1668–87. However, it has been conclusively demonstrated that these types are actually the work of Nicholas Kis (1650–1702), a Hungarian, who most probably learned his trade from the master Dutch type founder Dirk Voskens. The type is an excellent example of the influential and sturdy Dutch types that prevailed in England up to the time William Caslon developed his own incomparable designs from these Dutch faces.

This book was composed, printed, and bound by H. Wolff Book Mfg. Co., New York, N.Y.

Typography and binding design by Christine Aulicino